Stuff I Wrote in College

Jennifer Marshall

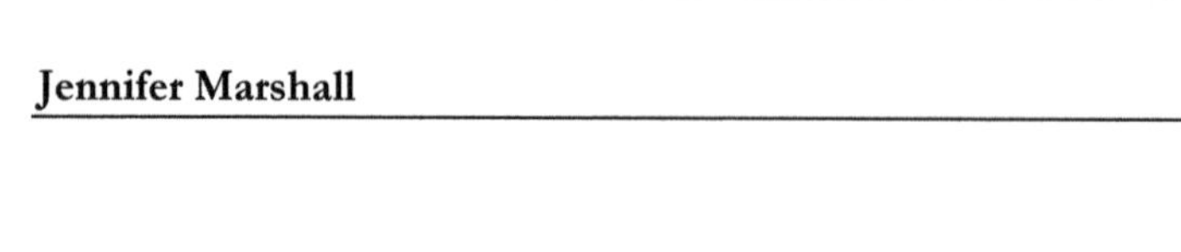

jmarshall@fas.harvard.edu

ISBN: 978-1-105-60155-2

Table of Contents

The following essays were written to satisfy program curricula for an associate's degree in human services management through Axia College of University of Phoenix.

Media and American Culture

Part One

Over the last century, news media has evolved from partisan print newspapers to investigative, round-the-clock digital operations—complete with narratives, photos, sound, and video. The changes in media include the methods of delivery. News reporting began with printed newspapers and followed along with the advancement in communications technology: radio broadcasting, television, and the Internet. Today, society can receive the news in a multitude of formats—print, broadcast, television, digital—and on a wide variety of devices: TV sets, radios, computers, and a number of portable devices, such as the Blackberry and the iPad. While modern media delivery certainly has the advantage of being accessible from anywhere and at any time, the greatest disadvantage of such accessibility is "information overload." Individuals may fail to thoughtfully consider one issue when they are inundated by multiple issues covered in dozens of news stories within the same short timeframe.

Another disadvantage of modern media delivery is the nonstop, unfiltered news channel that is the Internet. With anyone being capable of posting stories to the Internet, as well as the time crunch to "get the story" in 24/7 news media operations, reporters and journalists may fall more easily into the trap of quoting unreliable sources or even reporting fabricated details. The ethical and legal considerations in the online world include questions pertaining to credibility and trustworthiness. Beyond these issues, the online world is often a breeding ground for bias—and such extreme bias that it becomes libel. Though bloggers have been protected under the First Amendment, a legitimate news media operation would not escape legal liability for publishing libelous statements against specific individuals. The same legal considerations applied to traditional media should apply to nontraditional media. Until then, the Internet is rife with stories containing unchecked or even untrue information—increasing the potential for a well-meaning journalist to unwittingly report false "facts" and statements. Certainly, ethical and legal compliance in online interactions is of highest importance for the media professional in the online world.

Along with changes in media delivery and the issues consequently raised, another way the news media has evolved is in the adoption of a more objective position, as well as the acknowledgement of the media's responsibility within society. Journalists have moved toward the kind of reporting that is an amalgamation of objectivity and participation; though they avoid pushing a particular opinion, they recognize how the underlying issues of a story pertain to both them and the rest of society. Rather than simply report the news from a place of personal and emotional detachment, they seek out the relevance of the story in how it relates to life on an individual basis and how individuals can participate in advocating for positive change. The media still maintains its role as the public's source for news: its primary responsibility is to inform the public. As mentioned previously, the technological advances in society have allowed the media to report and deliver the news faster than ever before—and to report and deliver more news. Unfortunately, this may mean information overload for the individual receiving the news and undue pressure to deliver the story for the person reporting the news. In the case of a reporter who is caught fabricating sources and making up facts, the culprit may very well be an overzealous media itself. Would the reporter have felt compelled to be dishonest if the demand for immediate coverage had been removed?

As chief editor of the large metropolitan newspaper, I would have a moral and professional obligation to dismiss the reporter. There's no way I could continue to employ a journalist who had proven to be deceitful. I would assign a different reporter to cover the story again and ascertain the facts, so that when readers are informed of the false reporting, they can get the real story. Then I would write an apology to the newspaper's readers, explaining the incident and the disciplinary action taken and also directing them to an accurate report of the story, covered by a different reporter from the newspaper.

Part Two

Television, movies, and electronic games serve far more than entertainment—they influence and reflect the culture of society.

Movies reflect culture by examining issues relevant to society at the current point in time. Interestingly, even a historical drama would provide commentary on current social and cultural issues, such as a film about the Old West subtly offering a perspective on today's status with Mexican immigration or tensions between Christian and Muslim Americans. The relationship between movies and culture is exemplified in box-office sales and society's preoccupation with movie stars. America clearly loves the movies. Films offer escape from the monotony of daily life, its various hassles and struggles. Additionally, they serve as mouthpieces for the moral and ethical heartbeat of society. We find a position taken in movies, and one that we might choose to take in our own lives as we examine the issues and determine our personal morals and values. Movies affect culture because there is something idyllic in the storytelling, even when it doesn't end happily ever after. There are some explanations given and loose ends tied up, which may extend a minor sense of closure in our messy lives. Movies have the power to raise our level of awareness and debate.

Similarly, television shares in this relationship with society and modern culture within society by examining relevant issues and reflecting them back to the society in which they exist. Television acts as a mirror. Unlike movies, television shows make the journey from production to screen in a much shorter time frame. Whereas a movie might take two years from final shot to opening night, a TV episode is aired to the public within just a few months. This allows TV writers and producers to speak on more specific issues. Instead of addressing a broad topic like tensions between Christian and Muslim Americans, a TV show could address a recent news story about a group of Muslim students who were bullied by their classmates. Many TV shows—especially crime dramas—have made a regular practice of pulling their fictional stories directly from real-life news stories. Beyond the sitcoms and dramas, television now includes reality TV—whether topical, contest, or altruistic. Topical reality shows like *Jersey Shore* and *Real Housewives of Orange County* allow viewers to observe other people's lives. Contest shows like *American Idol* allow viewers to root for someone's success. Altruistic reality shows like *Extreme Makeover: Home Edition* emphasize the beauty and power of helping others.

Electronic games have often been targeted as the cause of teen violence. Certainly, many games are gratuitously violent and encourage immoral or illegal behaviors. However, there are plenty of ways that games have brought positive attributes into players' lives, as well as plenty of opportunities for the gaming industry to capitalize on an underserved market by creating more positive games. For example, *Rock Band*, *Wii Fit*, and *Dance, Dance Revolution* are among the most influential and important games released to the public in recent history. These games promote social activity and physical fitness. Since two of the more controversial issues regarding gaming are antisocialism and obesity—or, rather, the fear that gaming will lead to antisocialism and/or obesity—the gaming industry made a considerable effort to disprove such claims by the demonstrated success of socially and physically active games. Though complaints and concerns regarding the violent and sexual content of some games remain, the gaming industry is likely to steer the public away from this perception as it continues to produce more games with social, educational, and family values.

Happy Meals, Consumer Slavery, and Poverty: The Relationship between Fast-Food Advertising and Childhood Obesity

"A ¼ pound of flame-fresh beef, ripe tomatoes, crisp lettuce, creamy mayo, ketchup, crunchy pickles, and onions on a toasted sesame seed bun. It's America's Favorite Burger."

"You could say it's become somewhat of a cult classic, representing what's great about being anything but the usual."

"Maybe it's the double layer of sear-sizzled 100% pure beef mingled with the sauce and melty cheese, the snap of the onion and the tart crunch of pickle. Or maybe it's just that it's tall. Either way, you so want one."

These advertisements for Burger King's Whopper, Arby's Roast Beef Sandwich, and McDonald's Big Mac, respectively, showcase the ability of fast-food corporations to titillate the senses and tempt the appetite. Yet their words are nothing compared to their television advertisements, featuring glorious images of the sizzling beef, melting cheese, dripping sauces, and enticing condiments in a rainbow of color, as beautiful trend-setters and elated children delight in fast food's utter deliciousness. In 2003, more than 50% of advertisements during Australian children's programming were for fast food (Hoek & Gendall, 2006, p. 410). Much of the evidence presented suggests that immoderate consumption of fast food leads to obesity. With the increasing prevalence of childhood obesity, this epidemic demands consideration of its contributing factors and long-term effects on youth—including depression, poor social functioning, and low educational and career attainment as adults. However, this is not a simple matter of high-fat, high-sugar diets. Behind the cartoon mascots and kids' meal toys, a conniving industry has manipulated children with the illusion of happiness and left them in despair.

The fast-food industry has set itself up for consumers to be dependent on its products. Fast food's convenience and cost cater to modern American culture: bigger, faster, cheaper. Through advertising, fast-food corporations fight to establish themselves as the top brand of choice among fast-food consumers. In the process, these corporations are conditioning future fast-food customers: children. TV commercials showcase happy children enjoying the company of their peers and parents over golden fries and juicy cheeseburgers. Like Pavlov's dog, children come to associate fast-food with pleasure. Advertisements directed at children are designed to create this association, thus creating desire demand. Not only does advertising secure future consumption, it also supports current sales of children's meals—a child's pleading certainly has more power over parents than any of the fast-food corporations' billboards and commercials. Advertising effectively turns children into convincing spokespersons for fast food. With such clever marketing and manipulation, the fast-food industry surely knows exactly what it is doing.

These corporations cannot evade responsibility for the results of their actions. Hoek and Gendall (2006) stated, "We suggest that food advertising is not innocuous and that, in depicting frequent consumption and consumption of larger portion sizes ("up-sizing") as normal behaviors, it contributes to the rise in obesity that nations around the world have experienced" (p. 411). Perhaps it seems an overstatement that fast-food advertising could lead to childhood obesity. Advertisers argue that parents bear the responsibility of teaching nutritional behaviors to their children, guiding their media use and interpretation of advertising, and resisting children's requests to overindulge in fast food (Hoek & Gendall, 2006). "Even the most cautious parents cannot monitor their children's viewing behavior constantly, however," explained Hoek and Gendall, "and the argument that advertisers have the right to communicate with children, while parents must take responsibility for the consequences of these communications, is clearly unbalanced" (p. 410). Furthermore, parents may not be in a position to steer their children away from fast-food restaurants. Long gone are the days of the *Leave It to Beaver* family. With most households now dependent on two sources of income, and many wage earners working beyond 40 hours a week, parents are desperate for convenience, speed, and affordability—all of which fast-food restaurants serve. Despite their desire to safeguard the health of their children, some parents simply may not have reasonable alternatives to fast food. Accordingly, the frequent consumption that advertising depicts as a normal behavior does indeed become a normal behavior. With the greatest number of children now included in obesity statistics, commentators describe this growth in obesity as an epidemic (Hoek & Gendall, 2006).

The childhood obesity epidemic's far-reaching effects extend beyond adolescence and can dramatically influence the course of an obese child's life. Studies have identified the correlation between overweight and depression in adolescence and overweight and depression young adulthood; individuals with overweight and obese tendencies experience feelings of depression, debilitation, and degradation as a direct result of the prejudices they face (Merten et al., 2008, p. 1113). According to Merten (2008):

> Overweight and obese adolescents, especially girls, are less likely to enroll in college or even aspire to achieve a college or higher education degree. … The average obese woman has four months less schooling than a non-obese woman, and is 10% more apt to live in poverty. … Obesity has been shown to influence labor wages for obese employees compared to non-obese employees in several ways: lower wages for same job performance, fewer job offers for high-level positions, and denial of promotions. (p. 1112)

Merten's case study led to the conclusion that young adults who were obese during adolescence achieve a lower level of success in education and career and experience greater levels of depressive symptoms than persons who were of average weight during adolescence (Merten et al., 2008, p. 1118). Merten added, "Poor nutrition and exercise habits are not only detrimental to adolescents' health, but, based on findings from this study, also have lasting negative consequences for future education and career attainment, life satisfaction, and psychological well-being" (p. 1120).

Fast-food advertising's powerful influence and impact upon children cannot be denied, nor can it be ignored. Fast-food corporations use manipulative advertising practices to lock children into consumer slavery and long-term suffering. The marketing practices—eerily reflective of Pavlovian conditioning—capture children's loyalty, both present and future. Though parents aim to preserve their children's nutritional health, they have no alternatives that offer the same convenience and cost of fast-food corporations. Without comparable yet healthier options, many families succumb to frequent consumption of fast food, which is implied in the increasing number of obese children. Obese adolescents suffer long-term consequences, affecting multiple areas of their lives in young adulthood. A business is certainly entitled to take whatever ethical measures are necessary to improve its profits, but fast-food advertising to children is clearly not ethical.

References

Hoek, J., & Gendall, P. (2006). Advertising and obesity: A behavioral perspective. *Journal of Health Communication, 11*(4): 409–423.

Merten, M.J., Wickrama, K.A.S., & Williams, A.L. (2008). Adolescent obesity and young adult psychological outcomes: Gender and racial differences. *Journal of Youth and Adolescence, 2008 Oct; 37*(9): 1111–1122.

Race and Your Community

When I am asked to think of "people like me," race is not among the first several things that come to mind. I think of my age, my gender, my religious and political affiliations, my health issues, my employment status, and my income. Perhaps this is the byproduct of growing up in a generation that reviewed civil rights from a historical perspective and regarded racism as an outdated attitude, rolling our eyes as one might whenever a grandfather begins, "When I was your age…" In the 1990s, "token" minorities were a pop cultural must-have on television. It was cool to be black, and "white guilt" spread through films like *Higher Learning* and *American History X*. By the beginning of the 21st century, mentioning a person's skin color had become a social faux pas. To outward appearances, racism no longer existed in mainstream society. Racial discrimination had gone underground and become all the more contemptuous, for the subtle and silent racism left its victims disoriented and unheard. However, evidence of racial prejudice and its impact on human interactions can still be found in communities, leadership positions, and institutions such as the media and the workforce.

For the most part, members of my community do look like me. According to a report by the U.S. Census Bureau (2010), almost 85 percent of the Minnesota population as of 2009 is White, Not Hispanic. The second largest race group in the state—Black/African-American—only makes up fewer than 5 percent of the total population statewide. Persons of Hispanic origin come in close to African-Americans at third place, accounting for 4.3 percent of Minnesota residents, followed by 3.8 percent Asian, 1.3 percent American Indian and Alaska Native, and 0.1 percent Native Hawaiian and Other Pacific Islander. Additionally, 1.6 percent of respondents reported as two or more races. There are a lot of white people in Minnesota. Being white, I cannot recall ever receiving separate or unequal treatment from community members and leaders on the basis of my race. I have never felt unrepresented or misrepresented in work manuals or in the local media. In terms of race, I have nothing but similarities to the majority of leaders within my community. Because I am not exposed to racial discrimination or prejudice, I have no personal frame of reference for evaluating the representation of minority group interests in my community. However, I am considering the purchase of a home in an area of the Twin Cities known as North Minneapolis. This section of town is commonly regarded as the "ghetto," despite its many beautiful parks and clean blocks of single-family houses. I found that a group of graduate students in a psychology class at Metropolitan State University had partnered with a local agency—NorthPoint Health and Wellness Center—to identify North Minneapolis residents' views on their community (2006), including examinations of housing, demographics, neighborhood organizations, health and human services, schools, politics, media coverage, and parks and recreation. Despite a significant shift in racial and cultural composition of neighborhood population over the past 25 years, the increase in diversity has not come with an increase in economic prosperity. Not only have businesses closed or relocated away from the community, the students also reported, "Household earnings in many neighborhoods have dropped, while earnings city wide have increased. Poverty rates in some areas are 15-20% higher on average than the city as a whole" (p. 31). North Minneapolis fits the description of residential segregation. This segregation has translated into marginalization and victim discounting.

In victim discounting, social significance is determined by views on the victim's or individual's worthiness. Such inequity may not be surprising when stratification is clearly present, as it is in the short drive from the low-income neighborhoods of North Minneapolis to the multi-million-dollar lakefront homes of Minneapolis's southwest side. Attitudes similar to victim discounting can be sensed among the wider community leadership. "Community leaders who have vowed to stand by North Minneapolis do so in ways that can be construed as self-serving," the psychology students wrote, adding, "After the pomp and circumstance has fizzled—they vanish. They tend to come around acting like they are going to do something and then don't—adding to the growing distrust of community members in North Minneapolis" (p. 35). The situation is well summarized by the residents themselves:

> Participants emphasized the lack of adequate and affordable housing, the lack of access to employment and educational opportunities. They spoke of the lack of police visibility and of high crime rates and how these contribute to their sense of safety. They shared their views on the lack of involvement by community leaders and community members and were able to reflect on their own lack of involvement as well. (p. 34)

North Minneapolis community members went on to express their concern over perceived high levels of crime and real experiences of victimization. Here, genuine victim discounting becomes evident in local law enforcement:

> Several of the participants shared their experiences of victimization, attesting to the very real fact that current efforts to prevent and eradicate crime are ineffective. Their experience with those whose job it is to prevent crime has not been positive. In their eyes, there hasn't been enough law enforcement and that

> which has occurred has not engaged with the community. Rather, the community has felt as if they are targeted (e.g. prejudiced cops) or not taken seriously. Participants said the "cops don't care," the police do not support positive action in the neighborhood, and the police are selective of what they investigate; they don't get involved. (p. 31)

The perception and fear of crime in North Minneapolis is further perpetuated by the local media.

When community members spoke about the media's portrayal of their neighborhood, the subtly of modern racial stereotypes was called out into the light of day. "The media's portrayal of North Minneapolis has not helped," they shared. "People are afraid to live in their neighborhood and therefore don't get involved. The media consistently connects crime with Black people, which helps to create prejudice and fear of Black individuals" (p. 32). The media is not the only institution that perpetuates racial separation. The lack of schools in North Minneapolis has meant that children often do not go to school with friends from their own neighborhoods. But beyond North Minneapolis, a greater—and much more startling—inequality exists. A study from the Economic Policy Institute revealed that the Twin Cities has the widest unemployment gap by race in the entire country. "Unemployment among blacks was 20.4 percent … compared with 6.6 percent among whites," reported the Star Tribune's Molly Young (2010). "Blacks are more than three times as likely to be unemployed as whites in the Twin Cities, giving the area the worst racial disparity in unemployment among the country's largest cities." For those who would argue that the difference is due to education levels, the study itself settled the debate: "In the Twin Cities, African Americans with a high school diploma or GED were three times as likely to be unemployed as whites with the same level of education."

I did want to pretend that racism and discrimination had been removed by and large from the mainstream society, but I cannot deny reality when looking at the facts of the community near me—and the community in which I am considering living. This information does not frighten me, nor does it make me question the soundness of my interest in moving to North Minneapolis. If anything, I feel encouraged and inspired—motivated—to integrate myself in this community. Based on the listening session with North Minneapolis residents, there is a great need and desire for social interaction, community, and solidarity among neighbors in this area. I would like to be a part of that. I would be honored to do the little bit I can to move forward in unity and dignity as fellow human beings.

References

Students and Faculty of PSYC602: Principles of Community Psychology II. (2006). *North Minneapolis community listening project.* M.A. in Psychology Program, Metropolitan State University. Retrieved from http://centerforpsychologicalresearch.stasson.org/NMplsListen.pdf

U.S. Census Bureau: State and County Quick Facts. (2010). Minnesota. Retrieved from http://quickfacts.census.gov/qfd/states/27000.html

Young, Molly. (2010, June 9). Twin Cities has widest jobless gap by race. *Star Tribune.* Retrieved from http://www.startribune.com/business/96016354.html

Building an Ethical Organization

Human services organizations have a unique obligation to their clients. They are providers of services that directly impact the client's well-being. Therefore, a human service organization must be ethical. The highest standards apply for the sake of the client. Many times, an organization serves disadvantaged, vulnerable, or otherwise oppressed populations. The organization's ethical framework ensures that human service workers do not exploit or take advantage of their clients. Ethical codes of conduct also protect the organization. The ethical framework includes the mission, values statement, code of ethics, organizational culture, moral leadership, and ethical oversight. These elements are examined in the development of a new human service organization.

Description of Organization

This new human service organization provides household maintenance services. Services include cleaning, laundry, dish washing, organizing, painting, decorating, lawn mowing, and basic yard care. The clientele is persons on public assistance. Clients are recipients of Temporary Assistance for Needy Families (TANF) benefits, Social Security Disability Insurance benefits, or similar financial aid programs. All clients face considerable obstacles to maintaining their homes and to paying for traditional maid (or housekeeper) services. Whether their obstacles are time-related or disability-related, clients struggle to keep their homes sanitary and orderly.

This organization believes that one's home environment has a profound effect on one's functioning. Environmental chaos disrupts focus, time management, emotional balance, self-worth, and sense of self-efficacy. Restoring order within the home environment will help improve the client's overall functioning. For this purpose, the organization provides low-cost services. It is a nonprofit organization.

As a human service organization, this agency must be built as an ethical organization. Manning (2003) describes the initial step toward developing an ethical climate:

> First, leaders must develop an ethical framework. The framework is similar to a compass; it is used to guide "planning, decision making, and the assessment of performance" (Sims, 2000, p. 76). The ethical framework includes the organization's mission, value statement, and ethical code. It also includes the leader's moral vision.... The moral vision is the leader's commitment to a moral future that can be enacted through the mission and purpose(s) of

> the organization. Contributions to the common good, the environment, the well-being of oppressed populations, sustainability, and so forth are large order examples of moral vision. However, moral vision also includes the moral commitments connected directly to the agency mission. A final component of the ethical framework has to be the moral identity of the leader…that provides the moral commitment of the leader; the motivation to commit to "I want" and "I will" behavior, rather than just "I think" or "I wish." The ethical framework communicates to other stakeholders the organization's ethical stance. (p. 221)

Accordingly, the organization's mission statement is of primary importance.

Mission Statement

The organization's mission centers on restoring order within the home environment to help improve the client's overall functioning. In full, the organization's mission statement communicates its purpose:

"Our mission is to provide affordable, quality services in household maintenance; to support work–life balance for busy adults; to care for the domestic interests of persons with special needs; to create a home environment that promotes manageability, relaxation, and peace of mind; to foster relationships with family, friends, and community; and to honor fidelity, justice, honesty, autonomy, and service to the good of the client."

The mission statement supports the organization's ethical system, as Manning (2003) summarized:

> It [the mission statement] is meant to guide and inspire the overall direction of the organization's work and the program goals and objectives that are developed to do the work. The mission is the human service organization's contract with the community; it states clearly what the public can expect in regard to the population served and the nature and meaning of the services provided. The mission provides the community with a statement of the ideal end that the organization hopes to achieve through its work. (p. 204–205)

This mission statement identifies the organization's work and the population it serves. It is clear about the services' nature and meaning—promoting manageability, relaxation, and peace of mind, as well as fostering relationships with family, friends, and the community. From this statement, the public community can expect that the organization's services will be affordable and quality. The mission statement also sends a clear message about the organization's values.

Values Statement

The organization's mission statement includes a list of its core values, stating, "To honor fidelity, justice, honesty, autonomy, and service to the good of the client." Manning (2003) provides instruction for drafting a complete values statement:

> Similar to the mission, the values statement should articulate the essence of the organization that the leader(s) wants to develop and nurture. … The values statement should be congruent with the work of the organization, rather than a generalized listing of values that are important, but not relevant. (p. 226–227)

Thus, the values identified in the mission statement are expanded upon in the values statement. Herein, congruency is shown between the stated values and the work of the organization:

"We value fidelity. The client will receive the services promised, on the date promised, within the timeframe promised, and at the price promised. We value justice. Quality will not be lowered to equal cost; all clients will receive thorough attention and care. We value honesty. All service details and prices will be disclosed upfront; we will follow our agreement with the client. We value autonomy. Each client has a right to be respected as an individual with his or her own lifestyle choices. We value service to the good of the client. The client's best interests will always be our top priority."

These values inspire action by exemplifying ethical principles and their positive impact. An employee of the organization needn't experience conflict between the work climate and his or her own morals. These values also influence behavior by indicating general policy. Employees have a guide for how they should handle billing, delivering services, and treating the client and his or her home. This is an important element that Manning (2003) prescribes for an ethical culture that builds integrity.

> Sensible, clearly communicated values and commitments that articulate the obligations of the organization…are the organization's message to the outside world. … Values are part of the routine decision-making process and are factored into every important organizational activity. … Embedded reflection becomes part of the learning activities for all members as they consider, discuss, and disagree about the nature of the embedded values. … Systems and structures support and reinforce organizational commitments. … Leaders and constituents in the organization have the knowledge and skills they need to make ethical decisions. … All constituents who bring forward ethical issues, concerns, and challenges are encouraged, protected, and

> responded to. … The organization encourages ethical achievement rather than avoidance of ethical failure. … The organization avoids hypocrisy and incongruity between mission and policy and between stated values and behavior. (p. 228–229)

The organization's values statement relates to its mission by expanding upon those values in the mission statement. The mission "to honor fidelity, justice, honesty, autonomy, and service to the good of the client" is specified in the values statement. These values relate to the mission because they support the client's improved functioning. The organization can set an example through values-based actions. The client will gain an understanding of ethical practices. Perhaps he or she can then practice these principles. Such a response will further improve the client's functioning. One day, the client may no longer need public assistance. He or she will have been supported enough to finally be self-supporting.

Code of Ethics

In addition to the mission statement and values statement, the code of ethics is an essential part of the organization's ethical framework. The organization's core values must be clear to form the ethical code. Messikomer and Cirka (2010) warn that failure to clarify an organization's guiding values "increases the likelihood that organizational members will rely on personal value systems to resolve ethical problems. These personal values and the resulting behaviors may or may not conflict with organizational values, leaving decisions about ethical conduct to chance" (p. 66).

Therefore, the organization's mission and values are integrated and expanded in a code of ethics. As the *NASW Code of Ethics* states:

> A code of ethics cannot guarantee ethical behavior. Moreover, a code of ethics cannot resolve all ethical issues or disputes or capture the richness and complexity involved in striving to make responsible choices within a moral community. Rather, a code of ethics sets forth values, ethical principles, and ethical standards to which professionals aspire and by which their actions can be judged. (National Association of Social Workers [NASW], 1999)

The organization's code of ethics can be viewed as a public statement of its ethical position, rules for behavior, or a set of principles that guide professional and organizational conduct (Messikomer & Cirka, 2010). Thus, this organization's code of ethics, adopted from the *NASW Code of Ethics*, is as follows:

1. Staff respects and promotes the client's right to autonomy and self-determination.

2. Staff respects clients' right to privacy. Staff should not solicit private information from clients unless it is essential to providing services or processing payment for services. Once private information is shared, standards of confidentiality apply.
3. Staff should not take unfair advantage of any client or exploit clients to further their personal, religious, political, or business interests.
4. Staff should be alert to and avoid conflicts of interest that interfere with the exercise of professional discretion and impartial judgment.
5. Staff provides services to clients based on valid informed consent. Staff discloses fees and details of services upfront.
6. Staff ensures that fees are fair, reasonable, and commensurate with the services performed. Consideration should be given to clients' ability to pay.
7. Staff honors all agreements to service delivery, dates, times, and fees.
8. Staff uses accurate and respectful language in all communications to and about clients.
9. Staff cooperates with fellow colleagues and with service-referral organizations when such cooperation serves the well-being of clients.
10. Staff avoids unwarranted negative criticism of colleagues in communications with clients or with other professionals.

The code inspires a tangible outcome from employees through their participation in its development. Messikomer and Cirka (2010) strongly advocate involvement at all organizational levels in developing the code. Without this, "issues may not be captured, resulting in a product that is less useful as a guide for behavior as well as one that employees may view as irrelevant to their own experience" (p. 60). Commitment to the code is gained through engagement in its development process. Such engagement and participation also encourages moral behavior from employees. Most importantly, it supports "organizational culture building where people have an awareness of values, implicit values are made explicit, and everyday behavior is more likely to be positively impacted because the formal code is owned by the members and used to guide choices" (p. 66). The code of ethics will lack efficacy if it does not become a "living" code in the organizational culture.

Organizational Culture

A positive ethical culture is one in which the organization's code of ethics becomes a living code. Fostering this organizational culture is a top priority. Verbos, Gerard, Forshey, Harding, and Miller (2007) describe the objective's key components:

> Within a positive ethical organization, ethical practices are (1) modeled and promoted by authentic leaders; (2) infused through a positive organizational context in which formal and informal organizational structures, processes and systems are aligned with ethical practices; and (3) sustained and reinforced in an ethical organizational culture in which heightened ethical awareness and salient ethical identities among members contribute to a strong positive climate regarding ethics. (p. 19)

Important values, beliefs, attitudes, and norms are learned through organizational socialization (Verbos et al., 2007). This process imparts the culture perspective "necessary to perform organizational roles. Socialization is a complex, interactive process, and new members' proactive socialization behaviors, as well as leaders' active engagement, enhance the power of the process" (p. 24). In addition to orientation programs, formal training has been "recognized as the main source of socialization" and essential to new employees' ethical decision-making. Mentorship also plays a vital role:

> In a positive ethical organization, it is expected that mentors, whether in formal organization-sponsored programs or in spontaneous informal relationship, will act as role models of the living code, as well as increase the salience of protégés personal and social ethical identities, with the further expected effect of strengthening the living code and the ethical organizational identity. (p. 24)

Not only does this process communicate the organization's ethical culture, it also institutionalizes the organization's values. Employees, or members, are "motivated to seek self-enhancement and self-improvement" (Verbos et al., 2007, p. 28). Thus, the organization's positive ethical identity "provides a means to affirm and strengthen" the ethical identity of its members. With a shared ethical identity, members' goals will be aligned with the mission and values. These organizational objectives become "not only desirable but also achievable." As a result, staff will have more motivation, stronger desire to stay committed as employees, and "greater willingness to engage in cooperative and prosocial behavior" on behalf of the organization.

However, none of this is possible without the first key component of a positive ethical culture: authentic leadership.

Leadership

Vance and Harris (2011) assert that organizational transformation begins with the organization's leader. Leadership has a unique opportunity to inspire ethical culture. Transformational leadership empowers members to "do more than just come to work," as Vance and Harris describe:

> A leader should try to encourage inspirational motivation for employees through an acceptance of new ideas and by creating a culture of innovation and originality. Acknowledgement and approval of fresh ideas can help create a culture of motivated workers—and motivated, inspired workers have a true stake in their organization. A great leader can understand the necessity of facilitating ethical behavior in an organization and will take strides to do so. Employees want a leader who will be considerate on an individual level while also being fair. By creating a leadership culture of impartiality and evenhandedness, this can inspire members of the organization to take responsibility for not only their actions, but also the actions of the organization as a whole. (p. 17)

A leader's moral responsibility certainly is to uphold ethical principles. The leader must adhere to the mission, values, and code of ethics. By example, leadership develops and maintains the organizational culture. A transformational approach to leadership involves ethical conduct as a personal imperative. It inspires members to do the same. The transformational leader possesses a moral vision in which personal values and professional ethics will guide the organization's achievement of its mission. Such leadership produces reliable, consistent, and uncompromisingly ethical organizational behavior. The resulting behavior itself can be a method of ethical oversight.

Oversight

To measure the organization's performance in maintaining an ethical standard, the leadership can appraise employee behavior. A recent study by Valentine, Godkin, Fleishman, and Kidwell (2011) found that ethical practices produce more satisfactory performance:

> The results indicated that group creativity and corporate ethical values were positively related, and that both variables were associated with increased job satisfaction. Conversely, corporate ethical values and job satisfaction were associated with decreased turnover intention. … Evidence suggests that creativity is related to ethics because employees develop a stronger sense of organizational identity when they are encouraged to think creatively, and part of this identity is tied to ethical business

> practices. Another recent study also determined that perceived ethical values were instrumental in the development of organizational mindfulness, a construct that appears related to creativity and innovation. Thus, a corporate culture strengthened by ethics and creativity should work in concert to influence favorable job responses. … Further, ethical values should precipitate greater work fulfillment because it is difficult for employees to be creative when they are distracted and/or psychologically troubled by an unethical work environment. (p. 353–354, 365)

The organization can evaluate its commitment to ethical standards by evaluating employee behavior. An ethical environment is conducive to creativity. Creativity is conducive to job satisfaction. Job satisfaction is conducive to personal identification with the organizational identity, which is tied to ethical practices. In effect, employees are satisfied, engaged, and committed in an organization of positive ethical culture. When not performing to ethical standards, the organization's staff will have low job satisfaction and high turnover.

Ethical concerns call for oversight. Vance and Harris (2011) suggest, "Organizations also need to provide better internal mechanisms for finding and investigating questionable practices" (p. 18). For example, the organization could create a team of employees, similar to "a police internal investigations division, whose only responsibility is to investigate instances of misconduct objectively."

Still in its infancy, the organization perhaps should focus primarily on developing an ethical culture. Valentine et al. (2011) demonstrated that "as a company dedicates more time and resources to developing an ethical context, employees will respond more favorably with positive job attitudes and beneficial conduct" (p. 354).

Conclusion

This organization's values-based commitment is evident in its ethical framework. Clear mission and values statements are incorporated into a code of ethics. The code and its principles are institutionalized through the organizational culture. Transformational leadership, combined with moral vision, guides the organization's ethical culture. The resulting climate provides its own method of ethical oversight. With these elements in place, the organization can achieve its mission. Clients will be served appropriately, and their lives will be improved.

References

Manning, S. S. (2003). *Ethical leadership in human services.* Boston: Allyn and Bacon.

Messikomer, C. M., & Cirka, C. C. (2010). Constructing a code of ethics: An experiential case of a national professional organization. *Journal of Business Ethics, 95*(1), 55–71. doi:10.1007/s10551-009-0347-y

National Association of Social Workers. (1999). *NASW code of ethics.*

Valentine, S., Godkin, L., Fleischman, G. M., & Kidwell, R. (2011). Corporate ethical values, group creativity, job satisfaction and turnover intention: The impact of work context on work response. *Journal of Business Ethics, 98*(3), 353–372. doi:10.1007/s10551-010-0554-6

Vance, N. R., & Harris, A. S. (2011). Ethics as management principles. *Journal of Leadership, Accountability & Ethics, 8*(3), 11–21. Retrieved from EBSCO*host.*

Verbos, A. K., Gerard, J. A., Forshey, P. R., Harding, C. S., & Miller, J. S. (2007). The positive ethical organization: Enacting a living code of ethics and ethical organizational identity. *Journal of Business Ethics, 76*(1), 17–33. doi:10.1007/s10551-006-9275-2

The Tropical Rainforest Heritage of Sumatra

The Tropical Rainforest Heritage of Sumatra exemplifies ecological uniqueness. Its three comprising parks—Gunung Leuser National Park, Kerinci Seblat National Park, and Bukit Barisan Selatan National Park—are marked by breathtaking landscapes of mountains, lakes, and forests. Located within the Indonesian archipelago of Southeast Asia, the site contains one of the most impressively diverse biota in the world. It is an outstanding example representing major stages of Earth's history, significant ongoing ecological and biological processes in ecosystem evolution and development, exceptional natural beauty, and the most important and significant natural habitats for conservation of threatened species and biological diversity.

According to the United Nations Educational, Scientific and Cultural Organization (UNESCO) (2004), the Tropical Rainforest Heritage of Sumatra contains an estimated 10,000 plant species (more than 50% of Sumatra's total plant diversity), over 200 mammal species, and 580 bird species. Of these, at least 92 local endemic species are found in Gunung Leuser National Park alone. Bukit Tigapuluh National Park boasts "a complete collection of the entire Sumatran mega fauna" (Cocks & Bullo, 2008, p. 184): the Sumatran tiger *Panthera tigris sumatrae*, Asian elephant *Elephas maximus*, Sun bear *Helarctos malayanus*, Malayan tapir *Tapirus indicus*, Sumatran rhinoceros *Dicerorhinus sumatrensis*, and Sumatran orangutan *Pongo abelii*. Sumatra is also home to the world's largest flower (*Rafflesia arnoldi*) and the tallest flower (*Amorphophallus titanium*). The Government of the Republic of Indonesia (Indonesia) (2003) proudly declares, "For mammal species, the island has up to 201 species. As a comparison, Borneo has 222 species…. In relation to its size, Sumatra (476,000 km^2) is considered richer than Borneo (738,986.3 km^2) in mammal diversity" (p. 15). In addition to diversity, the mammalian population brings value in its distribution. Distributional factors offer evidence of geological and evolutionary history. The particular distribution of certain species—such as Sumatran orangutan and Malayan tapir—is explained by the Mount Toba tuff eruptions in the Pleistocene era of 75,000 years ago (UNESCO, 2004; Indonesia, 2003, p. 18). Studying the speciation of tropical plant *Cyrtandra*, Bramley et al. (2004) concluded, "During the Quarternary glaciations, the Barisan Mountain range remained an area of forest, acting as a rain forest refugium. The stable environment within this refugium is likely to have allowed the low extinction rates and gradual accumulation of species" (p. 61). Refugia sites provide evidence of evolution as well as long-term stability for such biodiversity.

The accumulation of species—the range of which Sumatra uniquely claims—requires specific ecosystem habitation and biological interrelationships. Befitting its diverse species, Sumatra comprises diverse ecosystems. The sandy beach forests, lowland rainforests, hill forests and peat swamp forests, highland wetlands, montane forests, and sub-alpine terrains are "supported by elements essential for the long-term conservation of the ecosystems and the biological diversity they contain" (Indonesia, 2003, p. 15). These essential elements include more than geological features; the interrelationships of plant and animal species also maintain the ecosystem's homeostasis. Ecoscientist Susan Lappan (2008) writes, "Animals may affect plant populations and communities through their feeding habits. For example, gibbons are believed to be important seed dispersers for some plant species, and some primates may act as pollinators" (p. 632). Lappan studied a siamang population at the Way Canguk Research Area in Bukit Barisan Selatan National Park. Like other gibbon species, siamangs "are arboreal apes inhabiting closed-canopy tropical forests" and "include new leaves, flowers, insects, and other foods in their diets" (p. 625), which primarily consist of fig and non-fig fruits. The study revealed that siamangs rely on flowers for food during periods of fruit scarcity. Lappan concluded, "It is possible that relatively high local availability of these important siamang plant foods is one factor promoting high siamang density in the study area" (p. 624). Posa, Wijedasa, and Corlett (2011) observed, "Peat swamps are also important for the conservation of a number of endangered primate species. The richest habitats for orangutans are high-quality swamp forests and lowland alluvial forests" (p. 53). The orangutans are fortunate; at low elevations within Sumatra, "two main forest types prevail: forests that grow on peat or on mineral soils" (Gaveau et al, 2009, p. 2168). This also bodes well for other species: "because peat swamp forests are usually found in an ecological mosaic with other forest ecosystems, they can provide resources for species with wide ranges and may be a sanctuary for species whose habitats have been altered by human activities" (Posa, Wijedesa, & Corlett, 2011, p. 53). Adding to the discussion on habitation affected by human encroachment, Mengersen et al. (2010) noted, "Typically, when [oil palm] plantations have moved in, the orangutans (and many other forest species) have moved, or been moved, out. Other forest benefits also disappear" (p. 106). Indonesia's own government (2003) best describes the dynamics of Sumatra's ecological interdependency:

> "The rivers and streams that flow from mountain slopes are living bonds connecting mountain and the livelihood in the lowland. When montane forests are cut unsustainably or land is excessively cleared for farming, ranching or mining, the water that normally flows into mountain watersheds washes over barren slopes. The

> resulting erosion transforms the promise of life, which is contained in mountain soils, into threats of deadly avalanches, landslides and flooding. As fertile soil and forests are lost, rivers begin to silt up and rare species of plants and animals face extinction. This environmental degradation threatens not only flora and fauna species, but also human." (p. 20)

Certainly, the relationships between plant and animal species become most obvious when they are threatened by human encroachment.

UNESCO (2004) reports that vast tropical rainforest in Sumatra was reduced to "isolated remnants" within only 50 years. The Government of Indonesia (2003) lists poaching, illegal logging, agricultural encroachment, and plans for road construction among the site's human threats. Returning to the peat swamp forests, a "substantial number of rare, specialized, and threatened species" have found sanctuary after human activity altered their habitats (Posa, Wijedesa, & Corlett, 2011, p. 53). For those species in the peat swamps, 45% of mammals and 33% of birds are on the International Union for Conservation of Nature and Natural Resources (IUCN) Red List of Threatened Species. Gaveau et al. (2009) summarize:

> "Over the last 30–40 years the high economic returns of Sumatra's lowland forest products and agricultural resources have led to consequent government and corporate investments in large-scale forest conversion to plantations, a pattern paralleled in Brazil. During the late 1970s, Indonesian Borneo and Sumatra changed from being highly fire-resistant to highly fire-prone during drought years because of the rapid increases in large-scale plantations and logging. Sumatra's increasing rural population of small-scale migrant farmers has continued to expand more deeply into the forest frontiers where agricultural land remains abundant." (p. 2172)

Thankfully, preservation measures exist. Gunung Leuser National Park, Kerinci Seblat National Park, and Bukit Barisan Selatan National Park—collectively, the Tropical Rainforest Heritage of Sumatra—have status as protected areas. Sumatra is also part of World Wide Fund's Sundaland hotspot. Additionally, Cocks and Bullo (2008) assure that the Australian Orangutan Project's funding of Orangutan Protection Units caused an end to logging and poaching within park boundaries. To further preservation efforts, the Indonesian government nominated the Tropical Rainforest Heritage of Sumatra for World Heritage status in 2003, explaining that the site's inscription would promote ecotourism, education, and awareness. The plan included outreach in the form of conservation education, bulletins, leaflets, pamphlets, speeches, discussions, and conservation clubs within the local community. In a

2009 study, "it appears that reducing deforestation inside Sumatran PAs [protected areas] has promoted protection to adjacent unprotected areas" (Gaveau et al, 2009, p. 2172).

Nevertheless, more work must be done. National park status does not guarantee conservation over a long-term period. Forest clearing and hunting still occur within protected areas, which are underfinanced and staffed by underpaid guards (Posa, Wijedasa, & Corlett, 2011; Gaveau et al, 2009). Future protective measures might include foreign aid to impoverished populations within Sumatra as well as increased funding for conservation programs. Local individuals can assist by participating and cooperating with biodiversity protection and conservation efforts. Other individuals may donate to Conservation International – Indonesia's Critical Ecosystem Partnership Fund. Also a viable option: taking a vacation to visit the area—ecotourism supports the Tropical Rainforest Heritage of Sumatra.

In conclusion, Sumatra's exceptional biodiversity holds significant universal value. If intrusion goes unchecked, much will be lost. Perhaps the greatest potential loss is a breakthrough in evolutionary science. "Even the most rapid presumed rate of speciation could not have produced local-endemic fish faunas within the few thousand years that appear to have been available at most sites," explain Posa, Wijedasa, and Corlett (2011), pleading, "Unfortunately, the ongoing destruction…means that such research will soon be impossible. Given the extremely restricted ranges of many of these species, their long-term survival is unlikely unless urgent conservation action is taken" (p. 54). With incomparable biodiversity and ecological secrets yet to be revealed, the Tropical Rainforest Heritage of Sumatra is a global gem. Untold benefits to humanity and history wait within the depths of its forests. We must protect and preserve it for the generations to come.

References

Bramley, G. C., Pennington, R. T., Zakaria, R., Tjitrosoedirdjo, S., & Cronk, Q. B. (2004). Assembly of tropical plant diversity on a local scale: *Cyrtandra* (Gesneriaceae) on Mount Kerinci, Sumatra. *Biological Journal of the Linnean Society, 81*(1), 49–62. doi:10.1111/j.1095-8312.2004.00283.x

Cocks, L. L., & Bullo, K. K. (2008). The processes for releasing a zoo-bred Sumatran orang-utan *Pongo abelli* at Bukit Tigapuluh National Park, Jambi, Sumatra. *International Zoo Yearbook, 42*(1), 183–189 doi:10.1111/j.1748-1090.2007.00031.x

Gaveau, D. A., Epting, J., Lyne, O., Linkie, M., Kumara, I., Kanninen, M., & Leader-Williams, N. (2009). Evaluating whether protected areas reduce tropical deforestation in Sumatra. *Journal of Biogeography, 36*(11), 2165-2175. doi:10.1111/j.1365-2699.2009.02147.x

Government of the Republic of Indonesia. (2003). *Submission for nomination of Tropical Rainforest Heritage of Sumatra by the Government of the Republic of Indonesia to be included in the World Heritage List.* Retrieved from http://whc.unesco.org/uploads/nominations/1167.pdf

Lappan, S. (2009). Flowers are an important food for small apes in southern Sumatra. *American Journal of Primatology, 71*(8), 624–635. Retrieved from EBSCO*host.*

Mengersen, K., Huanhuan, W., Wells, J., Buchori, D., Hadiprakarsa, Y., Nurcahyo, A., & Meijaard, E. (2010). The sound of silence: Listening to the villagers to learn about orangutans. *Significance, 7*(3), 101–106. doi:10.1111/j.1740-9713.2010.00434.x

Posa, M. C., Wijedasa, L. S., & Corlett, R. T. (2011). Biodiversity and conservation of tropical peat swamp forests. *BioScience, 61*(1), 49–57. doi:10.1525/bio.2011.61.1.10

UNESCO World Heritage Centre. (2004). Tropical Rainforest Heritage of Sumatra. United Nations Educational, Scientific and Cultural Organization (UNESCO): Paris, France. Retrieved from http://whc.unesco.org/en/list/1167/

Water Resource Plan: Sustainably Managing Marine Fish Stock

Overharvesting fish species—a serious problem for marine fisheries—severely reduces the numbers of species in the world's oceans. Data from the United Nations Food and Agricultural Organization (FAO) shows that "the world annual fish harvest increased substantially from 19 million tons in 1950 to 133 million tons in 2003" (Berg & Hager, 2007, chapter 11.3). Commercial fishermen harvest particular species—namely large predatory fish such as menhaden, salmon, tuna, flounder, halibut, and shark—to the point of excess. As a result, the fisheries become unusable for the marine species' food web as well as the commercial or sport fishermen's activities. The FAO (2001) reports 47–50 percent of global fish stocks as fully exploited, meaning that these stocks cannot provide harvest increases. A plan for management and sustainment of world marine fisheries is necessary.

Background

In a video learning resource, Berg and Kulesa (2008) refer to a study showing that commercial fishing has eliminated 90 percent of the seas' big fish. Jeremy Jackson of the Scripps Institute of Oceanography in La Jolla, California, published a two-year study in 2001 to trace many ocean species' decline over the centuries. Along with international scientists, he identified overfishing "as more destructive to the ocean than toxic pollution or degrading water quality" (Berg & Kulesa, 2008). In an interview, Jackson said,

> "The damage is close to complete, and it's almost certainly reversible, or at least mostly reversible. But what it requires is an utterly different attitude about how we use the ocean. ... We've fished many of these prize fish down to such extraordinarily low levels that I think we have to protect a third, or 40 percent, or in some cases half of the ocean from fishing for certain species." (Berg & Kulesa, 2008)

Berg and Hager (2007) state that fish species show nominal increase over 15 years following a fishery's collapse. At least three major studies, cite Berg and Kulesa (2008), have outlined the destructive consequences of overfishing. However, not all interested parties are convinced.

Commercial fisherman Pete Dupuis is skeptical of the studies, insisting, "I know this business, and I know it real well. That ocean is...very big. And it's going to take us a long time to really understand it"

(Berg & Kulesa, 2008). Governments face a significant challenge to solving the problem: authority. The open ocean does not fall under any nation's legal claim, thus circumventing any nation's legal framework and authority. Attempting to reducing harvesting, several countries expanded their jurisdiction limits further offshore. Yet many of these same nations give unrestricted access for all fishing boats within their national waters, threatening more than the prized game fish.

In addition to the fish species with high commercial value, overharvesting severely reduces populations of other species. This is particularly true for the animals that are unintentionally caught: known as "bycatch." Bycatch, as described by Berg and Hager (2007), includes other fish, dolphins, seals, whales, other marine mammals, sea turtles, and seabirds. Nearly 25 percent—approximately 30 million tons—of all marine catches are released and soon die, according to the FAO (Berg & Hager, 2007). Not only does overharvesting impair the prospects of commercial and sport fishing, it also maims the fishery's food web and the vital support provided to local marine species.

Still, Dupuis contends that commercial fishermen will be hurt the most in enforcing protections such as those proposed by Jackson. For example, swordfish produces considerable income at four dollars per pound, and Dupuis catches an average of a couple hundred fish—about 20,000 pounds at a potential total earning of $80,000. If one-third to one-half of the ocean were protected for certain species, as Jackson suggested during interview, then commercial fishermen's livelihood could suffer dramatically. In the same video learning resource for which Jackson was interviewed, Dupuis compared the proposition to fixing a leaky faucet by shutting off the water at the street. "And that's what the environmental community is doing now," he said. "Let's address the problem... And I don't think there's a commercial fisherman that wouldn't want to do that because we want to stay in business, and we want a renewable resource" (Berg & Kulesa, 2008).

Management and Sustainment Plan

In 2001, the FAO estimated that 25 percent of the world's fish stocks had not been exploited to the point that they could no longer contribute to harvest increases. "However," warn Anderson, King, and Martínez-Garmendia (2003), "any increase from these stocks would be temporary unless they are harvested under a sustainable management system" (p. 20). A plan for management and sustainment should include education, licensing and regulations, and fish stock replenishment, and be carried out within nine months (see Appendix A).

First, education ensures that concerned parties have received the same information. A public awareness campaign brings the issue and its resolution to light. Local agencies, such as counties' Department of Natural Resources (DNR), distribute educational materials specifically tailored to commercial and sport fishermen. Distribution locations should include marinas and establishments near docks and ports. Most important, a sustainable fishing education program will be a requirement of commercial fishing licenses.

Fishing licenses and regulations compose the second and third steps of a nine-month plan for sustainable management. After identifying issuing authorities for commercial fishing licenses in major nations of fishing industry, organizations should cooperate with local authorities to outline the licensing protocol and process. Ultimately, persons who seek a commercial fishing license shall be required to complete the sustainable fishing program. Law enforcement authorities and jurisdiction boundaries should also be identified. In the spirit of cooperation, participating agencies will form policy committees to draft and propose new fishing regulations and, where necessary, statutes. These regulations ought to include limits on catches of certain marine species within a given time period, such as per excursion. Once the legal framework is in place, DNR staff or other local agencies are delegated the responsibility of setting up checkpoints, similar to customs checkpoints in international airports. Here, catch limits will be enforced.

Lastly, and an ongoing operation, fish stocks are replenished via aquaculture. For cultivating marine species, the process is sometimes known as mariculture. According to Anderson, King, and Martínez-Garmendia (2003) mariculture produced nearly 13 million metric tons of fish—36% of the total production—in 2000. Aquaculture, including mariculture, "relies on various techniques to control the organism's reproduction, growth, and harvest" (Anderson, King, & Martínez-Garmendia, 2003, p. 14). A growing aquaculture industry, increasing from 2.6 million metric tons to 35.6 million metric tons over a 30-year period, presents a viable alternative to oceanic capture production. Furthermore, products from aquaculture sources ("fish farms") may be more beneficial: "increased stability of production and product supply, lowered consumer cost and increased product availability, and greater quality control" (p. 15). Additionally, aquacultural production is limited by the size of the cultivation area instead of the size of the natural population (Berg & Hager, 2007). Nevertheless, aquaculture is not without its own drawbacks, including pollution and net loss of farmed species due to carnivorous fish in the same habitat. A solution could be offshore fish-farming in the U.S. Exclusive Economic Zone's deep waters, of which the

National Oceanic and Atmospheric Administration (NOAA) is investigating prospects. Despite an alternative to the alternative, "opponents are concerned about the potential for pollution, the spread of disease, and the accidental release of caged species into the deep-water environment" (Berg & Hager, 2007, chapter 11.3). With appropriate operations and responsible management, though, aquaculture offers a sensible solution to the declining fish stock. First, fish farms offset the dependence on natural sources of marine species. As mariculture was capable of fulfilling 36% of the world's total fish production in 2000, it can surely provide even more if given additional resources and public attention. This would halt the rapid decline in marine populations. Next, emphasis on harvesting from fish farms will allow the wild fish populations to begin replenishing themselves naturally. Their numbers might increase significantly in fisheries that have not yet been fully or heavily exploited. Finally, fish farms cultivate marine species that are released into the natural habitat, thus guaranteeing an increase in population numbers.

Conclusion

Overfishing has wrought considerable consequences to marine populations. As yet, the problem has defied solution. Ongoing commercial fishing will surely result in the decimation of certain marine populations' remaining 10 percent. At the same time, halting commercial fishing will cause the collapse of an industry—along with its workers' livelihood. A viable solution must seek balance. Therefore, a sustainable management plan for marine fish stock is necessary. This plan ought to include education, licensing requirements and regulations, and fish stock replenishment, including aquaculture. Such a plan can be carried out in a nine-month period (see Appendix A). Following this plan will strike a happy medium between commercial fishing and marine protections.

References

Anderson, J. L., King, J. R., & Martínez-Garmendia, J. (2003). Chapter 2: Trends in capture and aquaculture production. In, *International Seafood Trade* (pp. 14–38). Woodhead Publishing Limited.

Berg, L. R., & Hager, M. C. (2007). *Visualizing environmental science*. Hoboken, NJ: John Wiley & Sons in collaboration with the National Geographic Society.

Berg, L. R. (Author), & Kulesa, T. (Editor). (2008). In E. Farris (Transcriber), Chapter 11: Declining Fish Stock. [Video Learning Resource]. *Visualizing environmental science*. Hoboken, NJ: John Wiley & Sons in collaboration with the National Geographic Society.

FAO (Food and Agriculture Organization). (2001). *The state of world fisheries and aquaculture.* Rome, Italy: Author. Retrieved from http://www.fao.org/docrep/003/X8002e24.htm

Appendix A

Table 1

Management and Sustainment Plan for Marine Fish Stock

Action Items	Action Steps	Timeline
Education	Launch public awareness campaign Distribute educational materials tailored to commercial and sport fishermen Develop a sustainable harvesting education program	Month 1-2
Licensing	Identify national issuing authorities for commercial fishing licenses Cooperate to outline protocol and process Implement required completion of sustainable harvesting program to receive license	Month 2-5
Regulations	Determine authorities and jurisdiction limits Cooperatively form policy committees to draft and propose regulations/statutes Set up check-points for fishermen to declare commercial catches (like airport customs)	Month 5-9
Fish Stock Replenishment	Oversee mariculture fish farms to offset dependence on wild fish populations, allow numbers of wild fish populations to increase, and replenish wild fish stock through release of aquaculture stock	Ongoing

Mitigation Plan: Energy Conservation

"Crisis" is the word most often used to describe the state of energy resource consumption. In the United States, skyrocketing gas prices and dependence on foreign oil are among the hottest topics, whether at the water cooler or on Capitol Hill. Attention is turning more and more to alternative energy sources, energy efficiency, and energy conservation. From hybrid cars and eco-friendly household cleaning products, to government programs and massive wind farms, innovators are cashing in on the energy crisis. The question remains as to how effectively these innovations have changed the national and global energy climate. Effective policies and regulations, technological advancements, and new alternative energies are necessary to mitigate dependence on fossil fuels, maximize use of renewable resources, and conserve energy.

Background

Renewable energy sources include solar energy, wind energy, hydropower, biomass fuel, and geothermal energy. For purposes of clarification,

> "Renewable energy property includes, but is not limited to, any machinery, equipment or real property, such as:
>
> 1. Equipment using renewable biomass resources for bio-fuel production of ethanol, methanol, and biodiesel, among others;
> 2. Hydroelectric generators at existing dams or free-flowing waterways;
> 3. Solar energy equipment used for heating water or generating electricity;
> 4. Wind equipment that converts wind energy into electricity; and
> 5. Geothermal heat pumps." (Cosmo Jr, 2011, p. 12)

Description of the problem

Many of these renewable energies are limited only by our current ability to harvest them. In some cases, like direct solar energy and hydropower, the technology is available but must be implemented on a large scale. In other cases, like wind energy, the potential of technology is underdeveloped. Berg and Hager (2007) propose that the full development of wind energy in North Dakota, Texas, and Kansas could meet the electricity needs of the entire United States—if there were new technologies to store and distribute the energy (Chapter 18.2, para.

15–16). While solar and wind energy are practically inexhaustible, some types renewable energy exist in limited quantities. Biomass, such as wood and peat, can only be used sustainably at the rate of its renewal.

In the international debate on sustainable development, energy is a key issue. Certainly, authoritative studies stress movement toward sustainable energy sources, as use of nonrenewable sources is a primary cause of current non-sustainability (Bagliana et al., 2010).

Human impacts and factors contributing to or affected by the problem

Though alternative energy is available, it is hardly mitigating the dependence on nonrenewable energy sources. As mentioned, the current technologies are underdeveloped. The implementation of alternative energy has not spread widely enough to have a significant effect on energy use. For example, of the 113.6 million U.S. homes using electricity, more than 60 percent are also using natural gas (U.S. Energy Information Administration (EIA), 2009). EIA data actually shows year-over-year declines in natural gas consumption from the past nearly two decades because of improvements in home construction and appliances, reporting "newer vintage homes, or houses constructed between 1990 and 2005, consumed 25 percent less natural gas for space heating, than homes built prior to 1990" (Office of Oil and Gas, 2010, p. 1). Yet space heating accounts for 82.4 percent of natural gas consumption in those 69.4 million homes—that is, 57.2 million of the total 113.6 million homes surveyed, or half of U.S. households (EIA, 2009).

Cultural factors no doubt contribute to the problem in adopting alternative energy. Lifestyle also contributes to the problem in estimating the energy needs that alternative sources should meet. As LePoire (2011) explains, "If everyone in the world used energy as the United States does, the rate of energy production would have to increase by a factor of four" (p. 35).

A number of factors are affected by adopting alternative energy policies. Bagliana, Dansero, and Puttilli (2010) list ecological, social, political, and economic repercussions. When a territory implements new energy policies, the flows of raw materials, energy produced, and energy consumed are redirected for containment; the arena of energy policy discussion broadens; and both private and public entities are attracted to the investment opportunity that renewable energies present.

Evaluation of current sustainability strategies and solutions

It is true that energy-efficient methods have been applied to curb energy demand, and solar and wind power sources developed to increase supply (LePoire, 2011). Perhaps the greatest contribution to alternative energy currently comes from state-level tax benefits, without which new renewable energy companies may have never started (Cosmo Jr, 2011).

However, current alternative energy strategies and solutions toward sustainability are susceptible to plenty criticism. Studying the effect of renewable energy policies on technological innovations, Princeton University's Yoon Won Song (2010) remarks, "I find that many of these innovations have not yet been translated into actual production of renewable energy" (p. 195). Despite the "strong regulatory connotation" of sustainable development, parties have not presented a consensus on the process, evaluation, measurement, and assessment of sustainability policies and practices (Bagliana et al., 2010).

Nevertheless, the EIA (2011) projects that total carbon dioxide emissions will decrease 0.3 percent annually between 2009 and 2035, from 19.1 tons per person in 2008 to 16.2 tons per person in 2035 (Table A18, p. 150). Total marketed renewable energy is estimated at an annual growth of 2.8 percent—increasing from 7.58 quadrillion Btu per year to a whopping 15.29 quadrillion Btu per year (Table A17, p. 148).

Bagliana, Dansero, and Puttilli (2010) argue, "Energy mix diversification towards the broader use of Renewable Energy Sources (RES) accompanied by a noteworthy reduction in consumption is an essential factor in pursuing the eco-restructuring objectives of society" (p. 457). LePoire (2011) adds, "A balanced portfolio of energy options and organizational support can reduce uncertainty and minimize the potential for surprises" (p. 38).

Plan for Sustainability

A successful plan for energy sustainability should incorporate beneficial practices and improve upon less sufficient approaches of current strategies and solutions. Mitigating dependence on fossils fuels, maximizing use of renewable resources, and conserving energy requires effective policies and regulations, technological advancements, and new alternative energies.

Action items, steps, and timeline

A 10-year plan is proposed (see Appendix A). This allows reasonable time for political and technological developments. First, partnerships with government are established. A number of programs provide grants and other funding to environmental and energy development ventures. The U.S. Environmental Protection Agency (EPA), for example, gives grants to various institutions for environment-related work, in addition to developing and enforcing regulations to implement Congressional environmental laws (EPA, 2011). Certainly, a relationship with this government organization would be especially useful not only in procuring funding but also in working with lobbyists and legislators to pass regulations. Regulations are of primary importance at this early stage because "policies that use quantity requirements have been more effective than price-based policies. ... Energy suppliers may supply more renewable energy if they are going to be fined for not meeting the renewables quota than if they are given financial subsidies" (Song, 2011, p. 195). Though regulating quotas is more effective than giving financial incentives, the monetary aspect still merits implementation. Tax credits should be provided because they have proven successful in nurturing new energy companies and encouraging investment in renewable energy developments (Cosmo Jr, 2011).

Second, the focus on business and industry should continue once regulations are in place, ideally by the end of year two. The plan outlines the steps for this action item as educating businesses on energy-efficient practices and objectives; using regulations, tax credits, and free market competition to advantage; and providing major national endorsements, awards, and other incentives for technological innovation. With this structure in place, companies might finally develop the national wind-energy grid that Berg and Hager (2007) had mentioned. New alternative energies may also arise. A diverse portfolio of renewable energy sources is indispensible in securing the future of sustainable energy (Bagliana et al., 2010; LePoire, 2011). David J. LePoire (2011), an environmental analyst at Argonne National Laboratory, foresees movement toward an impressive, new array of potential energy technologies. He explains, "Researchers are now testing new renewable technologies [such as fusion energy, space-based solar power satellites, Moon bases, and advanced nuclear fission options], with the aim of cutting production expenses, minimizing negative environmental impacts, and enhancing scalability" (p. 35). Elaborating, LePoire describes the development of an advanced, highly efficient nuclear reactor by TerraPower—showcased in a 2010 Technology Entertainment and Design (TED) presentation by Bill Gates—and semi-autonomous robots by Japanese company Shimizu to build a ring of solar cell collectors around the Moon's equator. The possibilities deserve exploration and the incentives to inspire further exploration.

Next, innovations must be implemented. As Song (2011) remarked, current policies have produced innovation without implementation. To remedy the disparity, a national public service announcement (PSA) should run in the media. PSA projects will educate society about energy efficiency and energy conservation. Additionally, these announcements will highlight companies providing energy-efficient solutions—an incentive and reward for energy industry innovators. Energy-efficient products are released into the marketplace at competitive cost. For example, Energy Star® (2003), established in 1992 by the EPA, "is designed to overcome may of the market barriers to the adoption of cost-effective energy efficiency products and services in a sustained manner and to help unleash the attendant savings for individuals and organizations" (p. 2). Consumers will also be offered tax credits for purchasing energy-efficient products and investing in renewable/alternative energy ventures.

Finally, a partnership with the United Nations will help in establishing energy policies and practices among nations. The plan advises aiding multinational, collaborative projects for advancements in energy resource technologies and management. Great contributions to global energy resource management and sustainability shall be awarded at the international level—a reminder that energy conservation is the whole world's responsibility.

Benefits and challenges of plan

This plan builds upon the experience of previous energy sustainability attempts. It makes use of the success in providing tax credits and enforcing regulations (Cosmo Jr, 2011; Song, 2011). It also seeks the development of a diverse energy portfolio, necessary for long-term energy sustainability (Bagliana et al., 2010; LePoire 2011).

Challenges include the uncertainty of energy projections, political climate, industry and society participation, and international cooperation. These challenges appear unavoidable, and should be offset by a diversity in energy resource options. Certainly, the exploration of new alternative energies, such as high-efficiency nuclear reactors and a lunar ring of solar cells, is very expensive. Here, a reminder of the greater good shall prevail.

Required government, societal, and global support

As indicated in the action items and steps, this plan does call upon the government, society, and globe for cooperation. Resolving the energy crisis cannot occur in a vacuum; it necessarily requires the participation of all who use the world's energy supply. LePoire (2011) writes,

> "These examples of potential new energy sources highlight an essential ingredient in the future of energy: the diversity of the organization involved in developing it. Some projects are government-based, such as those sponsored by the DOE. Others are collaborations between a government and an industry, such as the Japanese Artemis group. Some projects are sponsored by individual philanthropists and investors, such as Bill Gates and Vinod Khosla. And some, such as the ITER fusion reactor, require international collaboration." (p. 38)

Bagliana, Dansero, and Puttilli (2010) concur: "A similar need has also been acknowledged as a fundamental political and strategic objective at various levels: from the global scale (through the signing and enactment of the Kyoto protocol) to the community level, to various national and local scales" (p. 460).

It is hoped that the steps described for these actions will inspire and motivate the active cooperation and participation of government, society, and the world at large.

Conclusion

Resolving the global energy crisis is no simple feat. Even after shifting attention away from fossil fuels and toward renewable energy, significant consumption of nonrenewable resources continues. The renewable energies currently available have not been implemented to their full potential; the technology is underdeveloped. National energy policies have had some success, but much is still desired. Effective policies and regulations, technological advancements, and new alternative energies are necessary to mitigate dependence on fossil fuels, maximize use of renewable resources, and conserve energy. A successful plan for energy sustainability must call upon government, industry, society, and the global community. After all, those who use the world's energy supply have the responsibility to protect it.

References

Bagliana, M., Dansero, E., & Puttilli, M. (2010, June). Territory and energy sustainability: the challenge of renewable energy sources. *Journal of Environmental Planning and Management, 53*(4), 457–472.

Berg, L. R., & Hager, M. C. (2007). *Visualizing environmental science.* Hoboken, NJ: John Wiley & Sons in collaboration with the National Geographic Society.

Cosmo Jr, V. A. (2011). States provide tax incentives for investing in alternative/renewable energy products. *Journal of State Taxation, 29*(6), 11–64.

Energy Star. (2003). *ENERGY STAR®—The power to protect the environment through energy efficiency.* Retrieved from http://www.energystar.gov/ia/partners/downloads/energy_star_report_aug_2003.pdf

LePoire, D. J. (2011). Exploring new energy alternatives. *Futurist, 45*(5), 34–38.

Office of Oil and Gas. (2010, June). Trends in U.S. residential natural gas consumption. Retrieved from Energy Information Administration website: http://www.eia.gov/FTPROOT/features/ngtrendsresidcon.pdf

Song, Y. W. (2011). The effect of renewable energy policies on renewable energy production. *Atlantic Economic Journal, 39*(2), 195–196. doi:10.1007/s11293-011-9272-4.

U.S. Energy Information Administration. (2009). Table HC1.2 Fuels used and end uses in U.S. homes, by owner/renter status. In *2009 Residential Energy Consumption Survey.* Retrieved from http://www.eia.gov/consumption/residential/data/2009/

U.S. Energy Information Administration. (2011). *Annual energy outlook.* Retrieved from Annual Projections to 2035 via Projection Data page: http://www.eia.gov/analysis/projection-data.cfm

Appendix A

Table 1
Plan for Energy Efficiency and Sustainability

Action Item	Action Steps	Timeline
Establish partnership with U.S. government	• Procure funding from government programs (e.g., EPA) • Work with lobbyists and legislators to pass industry/organization regulations • Implement tax credits for energy-efficient and renewable energy property, development, and investments	Year 1–2
Facilitate industry innovations for energy efficiency and renewable energy	• Educate businesses on energy-efficient practices and objectives • Use regulations, tax credits, free market competition to advantage • Provide major endorsements, awards, and other incentives for technological innovations	Year 2–5
Assist society in adopting energy-efficient lifestyle	• Run national PSA promoting energy-efficient products and energy conservation practices (endorsing innovative companies (see above)) • Release energy-efficient products at competitive cost • Offer tax credits for purchasing energy-efficient products and investing in renewable/alternative energy ventures	Year 3–5
Coordinate international cooperation	• Partner with U.N. in establishing energy policies and practices among nations • Aid in forming multinational projects for energy resource advancements • Create an international award for contributions to global energy resource management and sustainability	Year 5–10

Human Service Administration Scenario Solution

As community needs change, human service organizations must adapt to meet these needs. An established nonprofit, community-based organization is facing one such situation. The local economy is depressed due to steady job losses resulting from employers relocating to other cities and communities. These other locations offer better economic incentives to employers. As a result, local property taxes that support funding of high school programs have declined significantly in recent years. The reduction has caused the local school district to lose significant financial resources to retain good teachers or fill vacant teachers' positions. Additionally, in the last two years the high school dropout rate climbed from 5% to 15%. The local school district, along with state agencies, decided to sponsor and fund new training and vocational programs for high school dropouts. In response to the increasing dropout rate of high school students in the local community and a worsening financial situation at the local school district, the aforementioned nonprofit organization is considering the opportunity to offer basic skills and vocational training programs in the community. The purpose of this initiative is to provide high school dropouts with necessary skills needed to gain potential employment opportunities. This organization has already established itself as a provider of high-quality educational, vocational, and training services to various segments of the local population. In consideration of this opportunity, the executive director must justify the reasoning behind this new program and develop a complete launch plan, including a review of environmental factors, a human resources initiative, and a budget.

Major organizational proposals call for a statement of opportunity: This organization has the opportunity to capitalize on its existing expertise and respond to an urgent community need. Through vocational and basic skills training programs, the organization can help the increasing number of high school dropouts gain employment in a depressed economy.

An executive director's vision is crucial in turning a challenge into an opportunity. In this case, the challenge becomes an opportunity by examining the impact on organizational structures, the environmental factors that pose risks or benefits, the human resources initiatives necessary to manage the strategic goals, and the budget profiles that achieve optimal allocation of resources. According to Kettner (2002), the executive director must have a solid foundation in management theory, communication skills, organizational ability, budget management, and attention to detail. In addition these knowledge-based qualities, the director needs values-based characteristics, such as consistency and reliability, integrity, commitment, persistence, and the able desire to empower others.

With an effective combination of knowledge and values, the executive director can identify and respond to the potential impact on organizational structures. Departmentalization, as seen in formal organizational structures, would be affected by adding the new program's responsibilities to each division of the organization, whether it is subdivided according to program, function, process, market, or client. The new program would especially affect departmentalization by process. In this case, each unit would undergo revisions to policies and procedures. Matrix organization, though valued for its flexibility, poses a different challenge. Here, the presence of multiple supervisors may add confusion and complication to the new program's implementation. The collegial model of organization would be profoundly affected. In this case, the new program is likely to fail; individuals have no accountability for accomplishing the collective work of the organization (Kettner, 2002). The proposed opportunity would affect a project team structure by requiring the development of a new team or team(s) to carry out the program's objectives. However, creating a project team structure specifically for the new program may be the most promising option. In Kettner's (2002) description of various organizational structures, the project team appears ideal for this program:

> A screening, assessment, and skill-development team is made up of workers who do the initial intake; gather education, training, and employment history; and get applicants into appropriate skills training programs. A job-finding team is made up of workers who develop contacts with employers and take responsibility for job placement once the trainees are job-ready. An employment-skills-training team is made up of workers who teach basic job skills including résumé preparation and how to complete a job application, and who secure donations for such necessities as clothing and alarm clocks for trainees who are job-ready. An evaluation and problem-solving team is made up for workers who do periodic follow-up with employers to collect data for evaluation purposes. This team also helps the new employees to accommodate to their new work environment and to manage the pressure of work and home responsibilities. (p. 98–99)

The opportunity to start the new training program may affect the organizational structure. An equally important consideration is that community environmental factors may impact the opportunity of starting the new training program. Therefore, the executive director must examine factors such as competition, financial resources available, and employment. Competition does not seem an issue because the situation has not been addressed by any other local organizations. Nevertheless, the opportunity is still open and available. The local school district, along with state agencies, decided to sponsor and fund new training and vocational programs for the high school dropouts. Because the necessary funding is offered, another organization could be preparing to capitalize on the opportunity. Total funding available for this program is $1,600,000. This factor is certainly worthy of consideration. At first glance, the amount appears sufficient for providing the new services. However, the organization would need to recruit and hire experienced trainers and other highly skilled technical staff to start the proposed program. In light of this, the financial resources available make finding qualified personnel a challenge. Alternative methods are necessary to attract new staff members. Employment is not just an internal factor; it is also an external factor. The local economy is depressed due to steady job losses resulting from employers relocating to other cities and communities that offer better economic incentives to employers. The organization must consider the possibility that even the most effective program may not produce the intended outcome; local employment opportunities may not be available for job-ready trainees. Given the aforementioned factors, risks include external employment factors as well as internal employment factors related to financial resources. On the other hand, benefits include the opportunity to fulfill an unmet need and the financial resources to provide necessary services.

In consideration of the limited financial resources for staffing, alternative methods are necessary to obtain qualified personnel. Here, the executive director can take advantage of organizational structure. As previously stated, the project team model is ideal for this job-training program. The project team is also useful in attracting and motivating employees. It offers employees a large amount of freedom and also a focus on the particulars of their specialty area. This allows them the opportunity to do interesting work and the chance to do quality work. Because each team renders direct service to the client in some aspect of the overall program, employees feel their jobs are important. Autonomy grants employees an opportunity for self-development and improvement. This intrinsic motivating factor is also served through communicating performance metrics and the framework for merit increases. Additionally, with job review criteria made available, employees are aware of what must be done to improve their performance and maximize their pay increases—an extrinsic motivating factor. Both intrinsic and extrinsic motivations are important components in quality performance within an organization. These are the two factors in Herzberg's two-factor theory of satisfaction and motivation, an "important study in support of the idea that motivation comes from the substance and structure of the job itself" (Kettner, 2002, p. 133). An individual's own improvement in competence, achievement, responsibility, and recognition are all intrinsic factors, meaning that the motivation is found within the work itself—and the individual herself. Extrinsic motivation is expanded upon in the performance appraisal and reward system.

According to Lawler (1977, p. 167), an effective reward system requires four necessary components: basic needs satisfied, competitive benefits, equitable distribution, and employees as individuals. Miles (1975) proposed a Need-Path-Goal Model, based on Maslow's hierarchy of needs, to accomplish the fourth reward system component of individualization. A manager would "attempt to (1) identify an employee's needs, (2) determine the employee's goals, and (3) establish a path designed to meet the needs and achieve the goal" (Kettner, 2002, p. 137). An employee's physiological and safety needs would be satisfied through regular pay and benefits, working conditions, job tenure, seniority, pension plans, and the like, as well as avoidance of reprimands from supervisors and managers. The path to connect these needs to the goals would be via meeting minimally acceptable performance standards. Social needs are satisfied by recognition from peers, esteem of coworkers, and acceptance by the group. Outstanding performance—exemplified in high commitment, effort, and regular improvement in skill and capability—allows esteem and self-realization needs to be served through promotions, recognition from managers, titles and status, pay, and challenging work, such as a job with opportunity for growth, creativity, and responsibility. To satisfy these higher needs of self-actualization, the effective executive director may implement the following managerial practices:

Supervisors' one-to-one interactions with employees are guided by theories of motivation, including motivating by meeting personal needs (Maslow, 1962), motivating by enhancing the quality of work assignments (McGregor, 1960; Herzberg, 1966), motivating by providing access to achievement (McClelland, 1961), motivating by reinforcing performance with rewards (Vroom, 1964; Montana & Charnov, 1993; Skinner, 1969), and motivating through fairness and equity (Montana & Charnov, 1993).

Accordingly, the organization supports the belief that employee personal needs ought to be considered when making workload assignments and that management does have a role in addressing the quality of work life and the quality of defined jobs.

Once the executive director has justified the new program through a statement of opportunity, consideration of organizational structures and environmental factors, and human resources planning, he or she should prepare the budget. The total available funding for the program is $1,600,000. Salaries and operational expenses have been determined. Projections indicate that 1,000 high school dropout students will be eligible in the first year of the program. In year two, the number of eligible students will double. At that time, personnel expenses (excluding the director and training supervisor) and operational expenses will increase by 50%; funding will increase accordingly. Also excluding the director and training supervisor salaries, cost allocation will be 60% to the basic skills program and 40% to the vocational program. Thus, a line-item budget for year one and year two (and thereafter) and a functional and program budget for year one are as follows:

Line-Item Budget	**Year One**		**Year Two and Thereafter**	
Revenue		$1,600,000		$2,287,500
Personnel Expenses				
Executive director	$100,000		$100,000	
Training supervisor	$80,000		$80,000	
Trainers	$500,000		$750,000	
Administrative coordinator	$45,000		$67,500	
Administrative staff	$75,000		$112,500	
Total salaries and wages		$800,000		$1,110,000
Employee benefit expenses @ 25%		$200,000		$277,500
Operating Expenses				
Rent	$125,000		$187,500	
Utilities	$100,000		$150,000	
Office supplies	$25,000		$37,500	
Equipment/lease	$50,000		$75,000	
Transportation and	$100,000		$150,000	

travel				
Outside consultants	$100,000		$150,000	
Overhead costs	$100,000		$150,000	
Total operating expenses		$600,000		$900,000
Total agency budget		**$1,600,000**		**$2,287,500**

	1	2	3	4
Functional and Program Budget (Year One)	**Basic skill program**	**Vocation program**	**Indirect cost and overhead**	**Total functional budget**
Personnel Expenses				
Executive director			$100,000	$100,000
Training supervisor			$80,000	$80,000
Trainers	$300,000	$200,000		$500,000
Administrative coordinator	$27,000	$18,000		$45,000
Administrative staff	$45,000	$30,000		$75,000
Total salaries and wages	$372,000	$248,000	$180,000	$800,000
Employee benefit expenses @ 25%	$93,000	$62,000	$45,000	$200,000
Total personnel costs	$465,000	$310,000	$225,000	$1,000,000
Operating Expenses				
Rent	$75,000	$50,000		$125,000
Overhead costs	$60,000	$40,000		$100,000
Utilities	$60,000	$40,000		$100,000
Office supplies	$15,000	$10,000		$25,000
Equipment/lease	$30,000	$20,000		$50,000
Transportation and travel	$60,000	$40,000		$100,000
Outside consultants	$60,000	$40,000		$100,000
Total operating expenses	$360,000	$240,000		$600,000
Total agency budget	**$825,000**	**$550,000**	**$225,000**	**$1,600,000**
Number of eligible students	1,000	1,000	1,000	1,000
Total budget per student	$825	$550	$225	$1600

Solutions to community challenges are not easy to determine. However, an effective leader can turn challenges into opportunities. A solution is possible. The knowledge- and values-based executive director identifies the potential impact on organizational structures, considers the role of environmental factors, weighs the risks and benefits, prepares human resources initiatives, and develops an accurate and manageable budget. With a solid foundation in management theory and practical application, administrators can lead human services organizations to achieve their mission.

References

Herzberg, F. (1966). *Work and the nature of man.* Cleveland: World.

Kettner, P. M. (2002). *Achieving excellence in the management of human service organizations.* Boston: Allyn and Bacon.

Lawler, E. (1977). Reward systems. In J. Hackman & J. Suttle (Eds.), *Improving life at work: Behavioral science approaches to organizational change* (pp. 165–226). Santa Monica, CA: Goodyear.

Maslow, A. (1962). *Toward a psychology of being.* Princeton, NJ: Van Nostrand.

McClelland, D. (1961). *The achieving society.* Princeton, NJ: Van Nostrand.

McGregor, D. (1960). *The human side of enterprise.* New York: McGraw-Hill.

Miles, R. (1975). *Theories of management: Implications for organizational behavior and development.* New York: McGraw-Hill.

Montana, P., & Charnov, B. (1993). *Management.* Hauppauge, NY: Barron's Educational Series.

Skinner, B. F. (1969). *Contingencies of reinforcement: A theoretical analysis.* New York: Appleton-Century-Crofts.

Vroom, V. (1964). *Work and motivation.* New York: Wiley.

Analyzing Financial Statements

Financial Ratios

Ratio	2002	2003	2004
Current	0.75	0.87	0.9
Long-Term Solvency	1.26	1.38	2.06
Contribution	0.53	0.51	0.49
Programs/Expense	0.53	0.72	0.77
General & Management /Expense	0.3	0.28	0.23
Fundraising/Expense	0.1	0.06	0.06
Revenue/Expense	0.98	0.94	1.11

These ratios paint an unflattering picture of XYZ Corporation in 2002. Its current ratio is 0.75, indicating that there are liquidity problems. Fortunately, the long-term solvency ratio is above 1.0, so the agency is able to pay annual expenses as they come due. With a contribution ratio of 0.53, the agency is receiving more than half of its income from one source. Regarding the ratio of program expenses to total expenses, the organization is spending only 53% of its outgoing funds on its program. This ratio suggests that other expenses may be too high, as those expenses take away from the agency's program. With ratio of 0.3 for management and general expenses to total expenses, the agency caps the threshold for generally accepted management expense allocation. As for fundraising, based on a line item for "Other" expenses, the agency is under the suggest maximum of 0.15. Finally, the ratio of revenues to expenses reveals that the agency spent more money than it earned. Reviewing the ratios for 2003 and 2004, the organization's financial picture shows improvement. In 2003, the most significant improvement is in increasing the current ratio and programs/expense ratio and decreasing the fundraising/expense ratio. Other 2003 ratios show marginal improvement; however, the revenue/expense ratio is more dismal than the previous year. The agency shows an all-around positive financial picture in 2004, when all ratios fall within recommended ranges (Martin, 2001, p. 56–59).

Fixed Costs, Variable Costs, and Break-Even Point (BEP)

	2002	2003	2004
Fixed Costs	$525,000	$545,101	$619,819
Variable Costs	$660,008	$771,580	$1,352,312
BEP	525,000 / (195–111) = 6,250 customers	545,101 / (182–113) = 7,900 customers	619,819 / (185–114) = 8,730 customers

Line Item, Performance, and Program Budgets

The purpose of a line-item budget is to control spending. It offers feedback about the allocation of resources for a fiscal year. Revenues and expenses are key features. A major advantage of the line-item budget is that it provides a financial guideline under which the agency operates throughout the year. It is the agency's basic financial plan. Line-item budgets also have the advantage of simplicity. However, the simplistic picture does not include how much service the agency provides or the cost of outputs and outcomes. For this reason, discussions based on line-item budgets neglect considerations about efficiency and effectiveness.

The purpose of performance budgets "is to relate agency expenses to programs by determining (a) a program output (or unit of service) performance measure, (b) the total program cost, and (c) the cost per output or cost per unit of service" (Martin, 2001, p. 85). These determinations offer feedback about how much it costs to provide a unit of service and how much service is to be provided during the fiscal year. Performance budgets pertain to the productivity of a program. A major advantage of performance budgeting—also known as productivity budgeting or efficiency budgeting—is that it determines the amount of service provided as well as the cost of providing service. It also allows discussions to incorporate program efficiency, instead of just line-item details. The main disadvantage of performance budgeting is the need for much more sophisticated cost analysis techniques than those employed in line-item budgeting.

The purpose of program budgets is to determine the cost of achieving desired service outcomes. Program budgets offer feedback about the effectiveness of an agency's program. Certainly, the major advantages of program budgets are that:

> "(a) they provide information on the amount of (client) outcomes achieved by a human service program and the attendant costs, including determination of cost per outcome, and (b) they raise the level of debate from service and efficiency concerns to client and effectiveness concerns." (Martin, 2001, p. 88)

As with performance budgets, the major disadvantage to program budgets is the difficulty in developing them. Furthermore, there are not generally accepted outcome measures for many human service programs (Martin, 2001).

Traditional and Nontraditional Approaches to Fund Development

Two types of traditional approaches to fund development that would be appropriate for the XYZ Corporation are foundation grants and "special" annual campaigns. A number of foundations exist, including the Bill & Melinda Gates Foundation that provides grants to a wide variety of human service organizations. Martin (2001) lists five major categories of foundations: "family foundations, corporate (business) foundations, general interest foundations, special interest foundations, and community foundations" (p. 175). XYZ Corporation can research the many foundations through several resources, including the Council on Foundations and the Catalog of Federal Domestic Assistance. In addition to foundation grants, annual campaigns are excellent, traditional method of renewing and acquiring donors. Special types of campaigns—such as dinners, auctions, raffle drawings, and dance-a-thons—offer an interactive, fun approach to fund development. The thrill of the activity often attracts more potential donors than door-to-door or telephone solicitation. In whatever type of special campaign, the agency can also emotionally appeal to current and future donors by having past clients share their success stories. The evidence of the agency's effectiveness would be confidence-inspiring and, consequently, generate higher donor revenues.

There are also nontraditional approaches to fund development that may well be advantageous to the XYZ Corporation. These include commercial ventures and social media. Concerning commercial ventures, the agency's clients could provide labor services as part of their mental health therapy. Many times, people suffering from depression and other affective disorders struggle with finding the energy to be productive. Lack of productivity, in turn, exacerbates their symptoms. By engaging in useful work within an encouraging, structured environment, clients are likely to experience improvements in self-esteem and general mood. Types of labor services might include custodial work and community services such as public property maintenance. These client-performed services would be contracted to third parties, and the profits would go directly to the mental health program(s). Perhaps the agency could even offer a discounted rate to participating clients. As an alternative to client-provided commercial ventures, or perhaps in addition to, the agency could contract its mental health services to other businesses. Such businesses may wish to offer their employees a "help line" for assistance with personal problems; XYZ Corporation could answer these calls, providing limited mental and emotional health consultations over the phone. Again, the profits from the contract would go directly toward funding the agency's programs. As for social media, this nontraditional approach is becoming a common practice among entities in every industry. By increasing its visibility through resources such as Facebook, XYZ Corporation increases its potential donor pool. Social networking ads will link to the agency's website, where site visitors can make donations electronically.

In conclusion, XYZ Corporation has certainly improved since 2002. As of 2004, the agency is in good financial standing, based on its ratios and having exceeded its break-even point. By continuing this trend, making prudent use of budgeting systems, and incorporating both traditional and nontraditional approaches to fund development, XYZ Corporation is sure to succeed in providing its services well into the future.

References

Martin, L. L. (2001). *Financial management for human service administrators*. Needham Heights, MA: Allyn & Bacon.

Creating a Social Program

The state of mental healthcare is in disarray. In spite of the prevalence of mental illness—affecting some 60 million Americans—the institutions designed to help have shirked their full obligation to the community. Persons with mental illness need access to compassionate, affordable, holistic care. At the local level, a human service agency with the necessary policy elements, financing, staffing, and evaluation methods can begin resolving this problem.

Problem Analysis

Mental illness affects persons from every walk of life. It is not bound by age, race, nationality, religion, political affiliation, physical health, or socioeconomic standards. According to the National Alliance on Mental Illness (NAMI, 2011), mental illness affects 60 million Americans—at least one in four adults and one in ten children. Despite the staggering numbers, many persons with mental illness do not receive the care they desperately need.

In some cases, the challenge lies in mental disorder itself. For example, manic-depressives are prone to stopping medication and other treatment during manic episodes, and persons with borderline personality disorder are notorious for failing to maintain relationships with therapists (a hallmark of the disorder). Yet, in many more cases, the challenge lies in the bureaucratic and capitalistic landscape of government programs, insurance providers, pharmaceutical companies, and health management organizations (HMOs). Chronic illnesses, including mental illness, are expensive to treat. Add to this the difficulty of treating mental disorder—wherein the client's own mind works against him or her, thus often interfering with treatment—and the result is a reluctance to dedicate the necessary resources to mental healthcare. Those who have a moral obligation to help are the only ones who gain by their refusal to adequately fulfill this very obligation. In the end, some 60 million Americans are left to fend for themselves; many continue to suffer and progress in their illness without proper intervention. This epidemic certainly warrants further consideration, efforts, and resolution.

Policy Elements

Mission, goals, and objectives

The mission of the proposed organization—further referred to herein as "Chrysalis Care Center"—is to transform the lives of persons living with mental illness. In setting goals and objectives, Chambers and Wedel (2005) define, "A *goal* is an abstract and general statement of desired outcomes, and an *objective* is a concrete, operational statement about a desired observable outcome" (p. 65). Chrysalis Care Center's goals are to see persons with mental illness lead productive, content lives; for both clients and staff to achieve self-actualization; and to positively impact the community at large. Consequently, its objectives are to (a) equip clients with adaptive coping techniques, (b) develop clients' vocational and interpersonal skills, (c) dramatically improve the general mood of at least 70% of clients based on their answers to self-evaluation questionnaires, (d) adequately determine through regular interaction how to best provide encouragement and opportunities to both clients and staff, (e) ensure the job-readiness of at least 50% of clients, and (f) supply the community with rehabilitated, functional, and productive citizens.

Benefits and services

To achieve the aforementioned goals and objectives, Chrysalis Care Center will provide appropriate benefits and services. Chambers and Wedel (2005) list nine types of benefits or services: material goods/commodities, cash, expert services, positive discrimination, credits/vouchers, subsidies, government guarantees, protective regulation, and power over decisions (p. 95). Of these, positive discrimination, expert services, and power over decisions are the benefits that Chrysalis Care Center aims to provide.

By virtue of serving persons with mental illness, the organization is providing positive discrimination—that is, a benefit "that attempts to restore equity where inequity has prevailed in the past. Applicants for the benefit are not treated identically or equally. They get special treatment now as a way of remedying unequal treatment in the past" (p. 93). Persons with mental illness are a historically subjugated group. Those whose illness has disabled them from effective functioning are protected under the Americans with Disabilities Act of 1990, which states:

> (6) census data, national polls, and other studies have documented that people with disabilities, as a group, occupy an inferior status in our society, and are severely disadvantaged socially, vocationally, economically, and educationally;

> (7) the Nation's proper goals regarding individuals with disabilities are to assure equality of opportunity, full participation, independent living, and economic self-sufficiency for such individuals; and
>
> (8) the continuing existence of unfair and unnecessary discrimination and prejudice denies people with disabilities the opportunity to compete on an equal basis and to pursue those opportunities for which our free society is justifiably famous, and costs the United States billions in unnecessary expenses resulting from dependency and nonproductivity. (42 U.S.C. § 12101(a))

As mentioned previously, the entities designed to provide help—government programs, insurance providers, pharmaceutical companies, and health organizations—have forsaken their sworn duties out of allegiance to bureaucracy and the almighty dollar. Discriminatory practices, such as the pre-existing condition clause in most health insurance policies and the outrageous costs of some medications (e.g., the antipsychotic Abilify, which retails around $700 for a 30-day supply), perpetuate the exclusion of mentally ill persons from "full participation, independent living, and economic self-sufficiency." Without such unfair practices, mental illness could be abated before progressing to the necessary point of dependence on public assistance, namely Social Security Disability Insurance benefits. Regarding the positive discrimination statement that "applicants are not treated identically or equally" (Chambers & Wedel, 2005), applicants to Chrysalis Care Center will be evaluated on the basis of their mental condition(s). Eligibility rules are discussed further in a following section.

In addition to the positive discrimination inherent in providing services to the mentally ill, power over decisions is a naturally occurring benefit of effective treatment. Though the classic definition of power of decisions refers to "the right to make decisions that serve the self-interests of the group with which the decision maker is affiliated" (Chambers & Wedel, 2005, p. 94), the benefit in this case pertains primarily to the individual. Nevertheless, the power to make healthy, appropriate decisions ultimately produces benefits to both the client's family and associates and the larger community. The client does come to recognize how his or her actions affect others, and begins to make decisions that consider the well-being of those around him or her.

Most importantly, attainment of the agency's goals and objectives require the delivery of expert services. These services are indispensible; without them, no program exists. (Program specification and staffing are discussed in later sections.) The "skilled, knowledgeable performances by credentialed professionals" (Chambers & Wedel, 2005, p. 95) develop the client's stress management, emotional regulation, and interpersonal skills. Goal-oriented work between professional and client guides the client's recovery toward a content, productive life.

Eligibility rules

Eligibility is determined by professional discretion. First and foremost, eligible applicants must be experiencing mental or emotional disturbance for which they are seeking professional mediation. Secondly, preference is given to applicants with a history of mental illness and/or a confirmed mental health diagnosis. This is not to say that potential clients with, for example, marital problems would be rejected. Simply, the agency's primary purpose is to serve persons with mental illness. If caseload permits, applicants seeking professional mediation in personal matters (i.e., grief, stress, anger, conflicts in relationships) could receive services. However, clients with mental illness shall always be given preference.

Service delivery and program design, theory, and specification

Chrysalis Care Center is a client-centered management system. Conceptually, its structure resembles an inverted pyramid or triangle, with a large base of clients at the top and the executive director at the bottom (see Figure 1, Appendix A). This system places focus foremost on the client. The structure is a reminder of the agency's primary purpose to serve those affected by the social problem it addresses.

The program's theory, design, and specification responds to the great need for a more holistic approach to treating mental disorders (see Figure 2, Appendix A). Many of the prevalent mental illnesses—such as affective (mood) disorders and personality disorders—both cause and are affected by disturbances in interpersonal relationships, employment and/or the work environment, and activities of daily living. This program treats the client's mental illness as well as challenges in resolving the aforementioned disturbances. The proposed outcome is a reduction in both symptoms of mental disorder and disturbances in relationships, employment, and activities of daily living.

Financing

Any human service program must determine the costs of staff, training, and salary; supplies and equipment; travel; rent or lease payment and utilities; and benefits and services for program recipients. A proposed fiscal year budget for Chrysalis Care Center is shown in Table 1 (see Appendix B). This budget indicates a staff of executive director, administrative assistant, receptionist, and three mental health professionals. Staff shall receive employee benefits, of which the total amount equals 25% of total salary costs. Training expenses are also included in the budget; this accounts for professionals' training and certification in advanced or specialized therapy techniques, namely mindfulness based stress reduction (MBSR) and dialectical behavior therapy (DBT), which are featured in the program specification (see Figure 2, Appendix A). Travel expenses of $2,000 are allocated within the program budget. This expenditure is to provide opportunities for clients, which may entail limited travel and materials. The line-item expense labeled "Other" is intended for fundraising and advertising.

As demonstrated in the budget, the agency intends to initially fund itself primarily through grant foundations. Solicited and unsolicited donations are also factored in as revenue; solicited donations are the product of fundraising activities, and unsolicited donations might include gift contributions from clients' families or clients themselves. Grants totaling $400,000 would allow the agency to reinvest a net profit of $25,000 into the program. Grantors may stipulate this reinvestment. If the agency receives no donations, the grants would still be sufficient to cover expenses and retain a small profit (again, for direct reinvestment in the program). An additional source of revenue is client fees. The agency hopes to see upward of 3,000 clients during the year at a standard rate of $30 per session (approximately 50–60 minutes). Compared to the $100 per hour commonly charged by psychologists, this rate is nominal and should attract a large client base. Provided that client numbers are as anticipated, the indicated revenue from client fees allows for a sliding fee scale. While self-support is a value to be encouraged in clients, the agency does recognize that not all clients are in a position to pay the standard rate.

Accountability for funds shall be ensured through careful recordkeeping and regular reporting, in addition to reporting required by federal and state law and any grant foundations that so choose.

Staffing

As mentioned in the previous section, Chrysalis Care Center's staff is composed of an executive director, administrative assistant, receptionist, and three mental health professionals. The executive director must possess intimate knowledge of mental healthcare needs. This knowledge is necessary to avoid many of the pitfalls in other health organizations, namely the tendency toward bureaucratic business over client care. Nevertheless, business and financial management skills are vital.

Therefore, the ideal executive director would possess graduate degrees in both business administration or health administration and psychology or human services/social work with an academic emphasis in psychology. Expectations include effective and efficient management of programs, finances, and staff. The ultimate responsibility for the agency rests on its director.

The executive director should have the assistance of the best staff so that operations and services are handled well in an autonomous fashion. However, autonomy does not negate cooperation. Regular, effective communication is indispensible as it allows for the coordination of services and also benefits autonomy. Staff members are better equipped to make independent decisions when they are thoroughly informed of the agency's current activities, objectives, and needs. By empowering staff to make decisions in their own professional judgment, the executive director has greater freedom to focus on a particular agency goal and objective: providing encouragement and opportunities for staff to grow and achieve self-actualization. A happy staff is an effective staff, ultimately providing greater benefit to the client.

A qualified candidate for the administrative assistant position would possess prior working experience in an office setting; at least an associate's degree in human services or social work (bachelor's degree preferred); familiarity with public assistance programs, financial management, and mental healthcare needs; excellent communication, organizational, and computer skills, and the ability to multitask. Basic job duties include maintaining financial records (incorporating client and payment records as logged by the receptionist), making budget reports to the executive director, assisting professional staff in researching and obtaining additional services for clients (e.g., legal counsel, health and/or prescription assistance programs, Social Security benefits, and public assistance for housing, food, and/or supplementary income), and supporting the executive director.

The receptionist need not have considerable prior experience in an office setting Qualifications include an associate's degree in human services or social work, friendly demeanor, multitasking skills, and a demonstrable ability to efficiently use office equipment, including software programs (Microsoft Word and Excel, for example) and machines for printing, copying, scanning, and faxing. The receptionist will screen applicants, schedule appointments, submit claims to insurance, propose payment options for clients with financial hardship, and maintain client and payment records. When necessary, the receptionist shall assist the professional staff and administrative assistant in locating additional services for clients.

Ideally, the professional staff would comprise a licensed clinical therapist, psychologist, and psychiatrist. The therapist can handle general therapy sessions, employing methods such as talk therapy, cognitive-behavioral therapy, and (if trained or certified in the technique) MBSR and DBT. Chrysalis Care Center will fund training and certification in MBSR and DBT up to $3,000 per fiscal year. The psychologist, having received more advanced education and training, is well qualified to handle cases with greater complexity and difficulty, including schizophrenia and borderline personality disorder. An advantage to employing a board-certified psychiatrist is that he or she is licensed to prescribe medication.

Rules for employees flow from the expectations of responsibilities and job functions. Therefore, basic rules for each employee are the fulfillment of his or her individual duties, as detailed in above paragraphs. Also as previously mentioned, effective communication is the watchword. Weekly staff meetings shall be mandatory. Other necessary rules include strict adherence to external regulations and laws, such as section 501(c)(3) of the Internal Revenue Code regarding charitable (nonprofit) organizations and the Health Insurance Portability and Accountability Act of 1996 (HIPAA) regarding healthcare fraud and privacy (among other subjects), and compliance with standards required by state licensure boards.

Evaluation

Success or failure shall be evaluated by fiscal performance and by client response. Budget reports will determine the agency's standing as a business venture. Clients' self-evaluation will determine the agency's effectiveness as a mental healthcare provider. At the beginning of the professional–client relationship, the client will be given a form to assess his or her current state with regard to mood, attitude and outlook, interests, sleeping and eating patterns, relationships, and major life activities (i.e., work or school). The assessment may be repeated at intervals in long-term cases. Upon closure of the professional relationship, the client will be asked to complete the assessment again. Marked improvement indicates the success of the services provided. Clients may also be asked to complete an anonymous survey regarding their experience with the agency. In addition to client evaluation, staff performance (especially that of the administrative/office staff) will be monitored by the executive director, whose responsibility is address and cooperatively correct any performance issues.

Despite the fragmented mental healthcare system in America today, mental illness can be effectively treated without undue hardship to the client. Such an undertaking starts at the local level to produce verifiable results, and requires a well-designed human service agency. The proper policy elements—mission, goals, objectives, benefits and services, eligibility rules, service delivery, and program theory, design, and specification—are the foundation of the organization. A solid financial plan provides the framework, and a qualified staff, with clear and appropriate rules, is the support. Like meter readings, a method of evaluation assesses the current level of outputs. Together, these quality components make a sound structure. Clients may then walk through the doorway to freedom from the bondage of mental illness.

References

Americans with Disabilities Act of 1990 § 2, 42 U.S.C. § 12101 (2008). Retrieved from http://www.ada.gov/pubs/adastatute08.htm

Chambers, D. E., & Wedel, K. R. (2005). *Social policy and social programs: A method for the practical public policy analyst* (4th ed.). Boston, MA: Allyn & Bacon.

National Alliance on Mental Illness. (2011). About NAMI. Retrieved from http://www.nami.org/Content/NavigationMenu/Inform_Yourself/About_NAMI/ About_NAMI.htm

Appendix A

Figure 1

Service Delivery System Structure

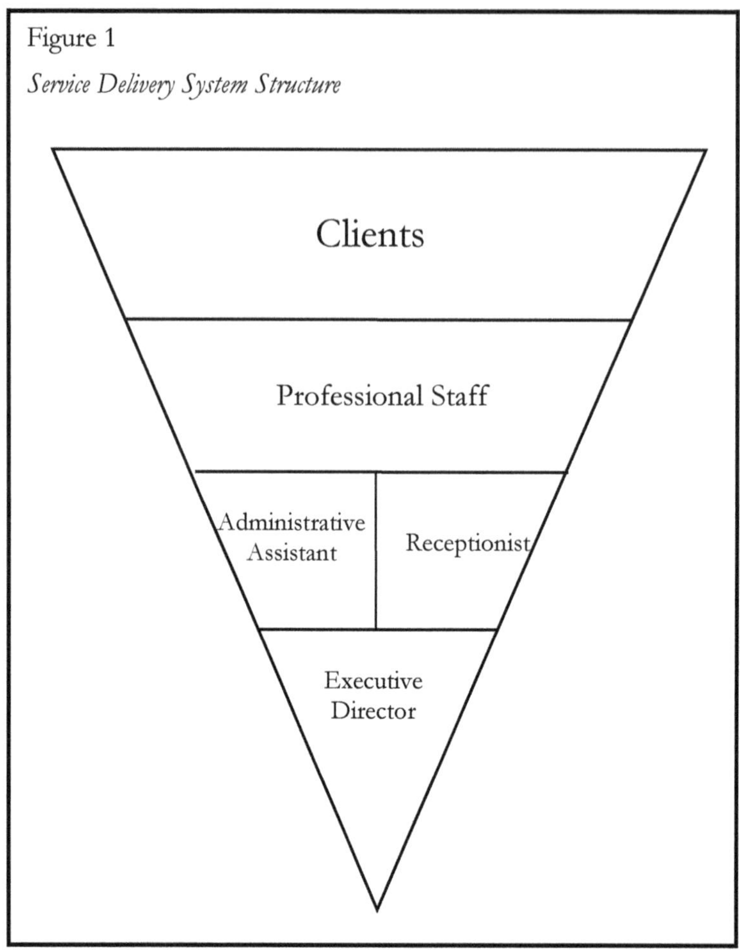

Figure 2

Program Theory, Design, and Specification

I. Program theory
   (a) Mental illness interferes with relationships, employment, and activities of daily living (e.g., bathing, dressing, eating, sleeping).
      1. Disturbances in relationships, employment, and activities of daily living exacerbate symptoms of mental disorders.

II. Program design
   (a) Providing traditional mental health treatment
      1. Psychotherapy
      2. Pharmacology
   (b) Teaching interpersonal and stress management skills
   (c) Structuring an environment to promote self-care and activities of daily living

III. Program specification
   (a) Traditional mental health treatment
      1. Administered by licensed therapists and psychiatrists:
      2. Psychotherapy—cognitive therapy, dialectical behavioral therapy, etc.
      3. Pharmacology, with referrals to prescription assistance providers and/or plans
   (b) Interpersonal and stress management skills
      1. Mindfulness Based Stress Reduction—facilitated by licensed therapist with professional training and/or certification in MBSR
      2. Dialectical Behavior Therapy—facilitated by licensed therapist with professional training and/or certification in DBT
      3. Active listening
      4. Boundaries
      5. Organization and time management
      6. Self-soothing techniques (e.g., Mindfulness Based Stress Reduction, breathing, counting, exercise, support networks)
   (c) Personal management
      1. Plan for environmental restructuring (i.e., a clean and organized living space that is conducive to healthy self-image and behavioral practices)
      2. Positive reinforcement—plan, rewards, and schedule of reinforcement / rewards to be developed cooperatively by counselor and client

Appendix B

Table 1
Budget for Fiscal Year

Revenue	
Foundation Grants	$400,000.00
Client Fees	$70,000.00
Donations	
Solicited	$20,000.00
Unsolicited	$1,500.00
Total Revenue	$491,500.00
Expenses	
Program	
3 Professionals	$180,000.00
Supplies	$2,000.00
Travel	$2,000.00
Rent	$24,000.00
Utilities	$6,000.00
Equipment	$5,000.00
Supplies	$2,000.00
Staff	
Executive Director	$75,000.00
Administrative Assistant	$45,000.00
Receptionist	$30,000.00
Training	$3,000.00
Benefits	$82,500.00
Other	$10,000.00
Total Expenses	$466,500.00
Net Income	$25,000.00

www.ingramcontent.com/pod-product-compliance
Ingram Content Group UK Ltd.
Pitfield, Milton Keynes, MK11 3LW, UK
UKHW041917190726
13854UKWH00003B/1285